Praise for *No Bad*

"An enormous gift—transformative, compassionate, and wise. These simple and brilliant teachings will open your mind and free your spirit and your heart."

JACK KORNFIELD, PHD
author of *A Path with Heart*

"Internal Family Systems (IFS) therapy, and the understanding that we all contain valuable parts that are forced into extreme roles to deal with pain and disappointment, has been one of the great advances in trauma therapy. Understanding the role they have played in our survival and being able to unburden the original traumas leads to self-compassion and inner harmony. The notion that all of our parts are welcome is truly revolutionary and opens up a path to self-acceptance and self-leadership. IFS is one of the cornerstones of effective and lasting trauma therapy."

BESSEL VAN DER KOLK, MD
author of *The Body Keeps the Score*

"In this trim and highly readable volume, Dr. Richard Schwartz articulates and deftly illustrates his Internal Family Systems model, one of the most innovative, intuitive, comprehensive, and transformational therapies to have emerged in the present century."

GABOR MATÉ, MD
author of *In the Realm of Hungry Ghosts: Close Encounters with Addiction*

"With our culture abuzz about the importance of self-love, world peace, spiritual awakening, and healing, few seem to offer the 'how.' How do we love parts of ourselves that hurt ourselves or others? How do we resolve our inner conflicts so we can participate in healing a divided world? How do we awaken to the divine within ourselves without bypassing our humanity? How do we heal trauma—and the chronic physical and mental illnesses it can cause? Without the how, we wind up feeling helpless to live in alignment with the core values and desire for optimal health that most of us espouse. Well, wait no longer. This book offers the 'hows' we've all been waiting for, sensible solutions that help you open your heart to even your most destructive 'parts' so that your divine Self can extend compassion to them while leading the way to wholeness. Internal Family Systems is a total game changer. I'm not exaggerating when I say this may be the most transformational book you'll ever read."

LISSA RANKIN, MD
New York Times bestselling author of *Mind Over Medicine*

"Since Freud, therapy has referenced and worked with the psyche as having parts, but Richard Schwartz has raised the concept to a magisterial art form. His claim that all parts, no matter how misguided, serve a purpose and should be met with compassion rather than antagonism is little short of a revolution. *No Bad Parts* is, I believe, his clearest, most comprehensive, and most inspiring manifesto. Anyone interested in IFS, indeed anyone interested in a happier, less conflicted life, should devour this life-changing, pioneering work."

TERRY REAL
author of *The New Rules of Marriage*

"Internal Family Systems offers a highly effective, hopeful, and uplifting paradigm for understanding and healing wounds that is revolutionizing psychotherapy. In this well-written book, Richard Schwartz offers the basics of IFS, a series of exercises to help you learn to relate in an open and compassionate way to all—even your most dreaded and extreme—inner parts, and the fascinating spiritual implications of IFS. This approach will change everything about how you relate to yourself and to others!"

DIANE POOLE HELLER, PHD
author of *The Power of Attachment*

"Do you want to be wiser, more compassionate, at peace with yourself, and more deeply connected to others? This book will show you how. Drawing on decades of clinical experience and contemplative practice, Dr. Schwartz offers a powerful, practical, step-by-step approach to healing past injuries and uncovering our innate capacity for love, clarity, warmth, and sanity. It's a must-read for anyone wanting to live a richer, freer, more joyous and connected life."

RONALD D. SIEGEL, PSYD
assistant professor of psychology, part time, Harvard Medical School,
and author of *The Mindfulness Solution: Everyday Practices for Everyday Problems*

No Bad Parts

RICHARD C. SCHWARTZ, PhD

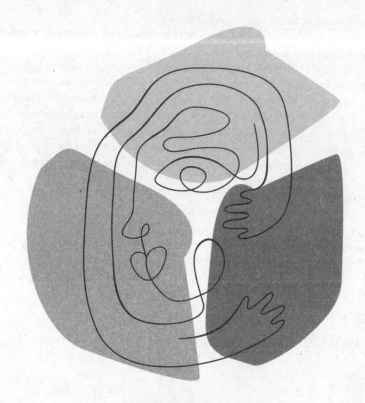

Healing Trauma &
Restoring Wholeness with
**THE INTERNAL FAMILY
SYSTEMS MODEL**

No Bad Parts

sounds true
BOULDER, COLORADO

Sounds True
Boulder, CO 80306

This book is not intended as a substitute for the medical recommendations of physicians, mental health professionals, or other health-care providers. Rather, it is
intended to offer information to help the reader cooperate with physicians, mental
health professionals, and health-care providers in a mutual quest for optimum
well-being. We advise readers to carefully review and understand the ideas presented
and to seek the advice of a qualified professional before attempting to use them.

Published 2021

Cover design by Lisa Kerans
Book design by Linsey Dodaro

FSC
www.fsc.org
MIX
Paper | Supporting
responsible forestry
FSC® C103098

Printed in the United States of America

BK06046

Library of Congress Cataloging-in-Publication Data

Names: Schwartz, Richard C., author.
Title: No bad parts : healing trauma and restoring wholeness with the internal
  family systems model / Richard C. Schwartz.
Description: Boulder, Colorado : Sounds True, 2021. | Includes
  bibliographical references.
Identifiers: LCCN 2020041452 (print) | LCCN 2020041453 (ebook) | ISBN
  9781683646686 (paperback) | ISBN 9781683646693 (ebook)
Subjects: LCSH: Psychotherapy. | Personality.
Classification: LCC RC480 .S334 2021 (print) | LCC RC480 (ebook) | DDC
  616.89/14--dc23
LC record available at https://lccn.loc.gov/2020041452
LC ebook record available at https://lccn.loc.gov/2020041453

If a factory is torn down but the rationality that produced it is left
standing, then that rationality will simply produce another factory.
If a revolution destroys a government but the patterns
of thought that produced the government are left intact,
then those patterns will repeat themselves.[1]

ROBERT PIRSIG

I used to think the top environmental problems were biodiversity
loss, ecosystem collapse, and climate change. I thought that
thirty years of good science could address these problems. I was
wrong. The top environmental problems are selfishness, greed,
and apathy, and to deal with those we need a cultural and spiritual
transformation. And we scientists don't know how to do that.[2]

GUS SPETH

Then it was as if I suddenly saw the secret beauty of their hearts,
the depth of their hearts where neither sin nor desire nor self-
knowledge can reach, the core of their reality, the person that each
one is in God's eyes. If only they could all see themselves as they
really are. If only we could see each other that way all the time.
There would be no more war, no more hatred, no more cruelty,
no more greed. . . . I suppose the big problem would be
that we would fall down and worship each other.[3]

THOMAS MERTON

CONTENTS

FOREWORD

I remember the moment I was formally introduced to Dick Schwartz's Internal Family Systems (IFS) work. I had flown to Asheville, North Carolina, in the midst of a second bout of postpartum depression to address the many underpinnings of my overwork, over-giving, and chronic overextension. This lifestyle has become increasingly normalized and celebrated even as it continues to wreak havoc on our physical, emotional, and relational lives. I was there for several days with Bryan Robinson, a seminal voice in work addiction recovery. I was deeply committed to looking at the elements of my internal world that kept me frozen yet frantic on life's increasingly quickening treadmill. I distinctly remember looking at Bryan at one point in the middle of a deep inquiry and asking him, "What is this, Bryan?" "This is Internal Family Systems," he said. I smiled at how graceful and deeply kind and all-embracing this work was. And how much more easily I could find my seat of awareness as I dialogued with many different parts within, some of whom have been yearning for attention for a very long time. It was in doing IFS work that I found an anchor, a place of warm neutrality and curious witnessing, a self-compassion that had been nearly impossible to will myself into offering to my own psyche.

I have been a "parts girl" since as far back as I can remember. I have always been obsessed with our complex, fragile, multitudinous, and fascinating human condition. When I started to work with IFS, I was buoyed by the idea of returning to our birthright of wholeness through offering attention and care to each "part" of myself as it adorably, horrifyingly, ceaselessly, and sometimes painfully presented itself. It was encouraging that my angry part and my mother part and my artist part and my financially responsible (or irresponsible!) part and my free-spirit part could somehow bring wisdom to me if I but opened my heart and my curiosity to them. Each part—as scary or illuminating or mysterious as it may appear to be—could offer wisdom and solace and vision. I came to see these internal parts as messengers. Dialoguing with them could offer helpful guidance and insight. The whole system of my many "selves" could thereby integrate into my everyday personality and life. These parts could even dialogue *with* and *among* each other, facilitated by my highest Self. In doing so, there would emerge clarity, ideas, or answers to seemingly insurmountable, complicated questions about my life. These answers would come fast and furious as I communicated through words, writing, movement, and art with the many parts within, even and especially the parts that scared me the most.

In my internal world, I encountered my own murderous rage, my shame, terrors, depression, aches and yearnings, humiliations, and grief. In addition to these "dark" or "bad" parts that seemed to want to doom me to repeated patterns and painful habits, there were equally "light" or "good" parts that also required my courage to open to the visionary parts; the generous parts; the intelligent parts; the leadership parts; the gifted, sensitive, empathic parts. Some parts seemed easier to dialogue with than others. Some felt riskier and downright threatening to embrace. The deeper I went into Dick's IFS work, the more his words and teaching rang liberatingly true. That each part, however harrowing its acting-out, however hidden, confusing, or painful, had the best of intentions and held helpful messages for me. Without fail, *each* part, whether an exile, manager, or protector, had profoundly kind and wise insights for me from my highest Self, if I but took the time to be there with them.

In the process of becoming more and more familiar with IFS, a rich sense of spirituality emerged. It was the soulful reward for allowing this curiosity to ever so slowly open up my bound heart. I saw that this Self that dialogues with all the egoic parts *is* my/the soul. Dwelling in this awareness allowed me to have a direct, physically felt sense of god/love/spirit/compassion. I came to see that the true dialogue began when I found this "seat" of Self. I would recognize it when I would begin to feel the agendaless-ness of the IFS "eight Cs": creativity, courage, curiosity, a sense of connection, compassion, clarity, calm, confidence. What had felt daunting to me my whole life—going within to take responsibility for or inquire about my urges, compulsions, triggers, and reactions—slowly became somewhat exciting. Dick Schwartz took all the Jungian and shadow work I have done to a whole other level of healing.

I am very grateful that Dick has continued to spread the word of IFS around the world. Watching him do IFS work with people is a heartwarming and deeply connective sight to behold. I believe we need IFS now more than ever before. His work offers each of us nothing less than the cultivation of kindness, wisdom, and empowerment if we're willing to look within. Doing this work allows every single part of us a moment in the sun. In giving our attention to the parts that need it most, true healing happens. As the compassion grows within us for our very selves, slowly but assuredly it affects the world at large, supporting our efforts to grow and shift toward a world of less divisiveness, strife, and needless suffering. We see that our delicate and brilliant humanity is shared among us all.

Alanis Morissette
San Francisco, California
March 2021

Introduction

As a psychotherapist, I've worked with many people who came to me shortly after their lives had crashed. Everything was going great until the sudden heart attack, divorce, or death of a child. If not for that life-jarring event, they would never have thought to see a therapist, because they felt successful.

After the event they can't find the same drive or determination. Their former goals of having big houses or reputations have lost their meaning. They feel at sea and vulnerable in a way that's unfamiliar and scary. They are also newly open. Some light can get through the cracks in their protective foundations.

Those can be wake-up call events if I can help them keep the striving, materialistic, competitive parts of them that had dominated their lives from regaining dominance so they can explore what else is inside them. In doing so, I can help them access what I call *the Self*—an essence of calm, clarity, compassion, and connectedness—and from that place begin to listen to the parts of them that had been exiled by more dominant ones. As they discover that they love the simple pleasures of enjoying nature, reading, creative activities, being playful with friends, finding more intimacy with their partners or children, and being of service to others, they decide to change their lives so as to make room for their Self and the newly discovered parts of them.

Those clients and the rest of us didn't come to be dominated by those striving, materialistic, and competitive parts by accident. Those are the same parts that dominate most of the countries on our planet and particularly my country, the United States. When my clients are in the grip of those particular parts, they have little regard for the damage they're doing to their health and relationships. Similarly, countries obsessed with unlimited growth have little regard for their impact on the majority of their people, or the health of the climate and the Earth.

Such mindless striving—of people or of countries—usually leads to a crash of some sort. As I write this, we are amid the COVID-19 pandemic. It has the potential to be the wake-up call we need so we don't suffer worse ones down the road, but it remains to be seen whether our leaders will use this painful pause to listen to the suffering of the majority of our people and also learn to collaborate rather than compete with other countries. Can we change nationally and internationally in the ways my clients are often able to?

Inherent Goodness

We can't make the necessary changes without a new model of the mind. Ecologist Daniel Christian Wahl states that "Humanity is coming of age and needs a 'new story' that is powerful and meaningful enough to galvanize global collaboration and guide a collective response to the converging crises we are facing. . . . In the fundamentally interconnected and interdependent planetary system we participate in, the best way to care for oneself and those closest to oneself is to start caring more for the benefit of the collective (all life). Metaphorically speaking, we are all in the same boat, our planetary life support system, or in Buckminster Fuller's words: 'Spaceship Earth.' The 'them-against-us' thinking that for too long has defined politics between nations, companies and people is profoundly anachronistic."[1]

Jimmy Carter echoes that sentiment: "What is needed now, more than ever, is leadership that steers us away from fear and fosters greater confidence in the inherent goodness and ingenuity of humanity."[2] Our leaders can't do that, however, with the way we currently understand the mind because it highlights the darkness in humanity.

We need a new paradigm that convincingly shows that humanity is inherently good and thoroughly interconnected. With that understanding, we can finally move from being ego-, family-, and ethno-centric to species-, bio-, and planet-centric.

Such a change won't be easy. Too many of our basic institutions are based on the dark view. Take, for example, neoliberalism, the economic philosophy of Milton Friedman that undergirds the kind of cutthroat capitalism that has dominated many countries, including the US, since the days of Ronald Reagan and Margaret Thatcher. Neoliberalism is based on the belief that people are basically selfish and, therefore, it's everyone for themselves in a survival-of-the-fittest world. The government needs to get out of the way so the fittest can not only help us survive, but thrive. This economic philosophy has resulted in massive inequality as well as the disconnection and polarization among people that we experience so dramatically today. The time has come for a new view of human nature that releases the collaboration and caring that lives in our hearts.

The Promise of IFS

I know it sounds grandiose, but this book offers the kind of uplifting paradigm and set of practices that can achieve the changes we need. It's full of exercises that will confirm the radically positive assertions I make about the nature of the mind so you can experience it for yourself (and not just take it from me).

I've been developing IFS (Internal Family Systems) for almost four decades. It's taken me on a long, fascinating, and—as emphasized in this book—spiritual journey that I want to share with you. This journey has transformed my beliefs about myself, about what people are about, about the essence of human goodness, and about how much transformation is possible. IFS has morphed over time from being exclusively about psychotherapy to becoming a kind of spiritual practice, although you don't have to define yourself as spiritual to practice it. At its core, IFS is a loving way of relating internally (to your parts) and externally (to the people in your life), so in that sense, IFS is a life practice, as well. It's something you can do on a daily, moment-to-moment basis—at any time, by yourself or with others.

At this point, there might be a part of you that's skeptical. After all, that's a lot to promise in the opening paragraphs of a book. All I ask is that your skeptic give you enough space inside to try these ideas on for a little while, including trying some of the exercises so you can check it out for yourself. In my experience, it's difficult to believe in the promise of IFS until you actually try it.

PART ONE

Internal Family Systems

CHAPTER ONE

We're All Multiple

We were all raised in what I'll call the mono-mind belief system—the idea that you have one mind, out of which different thoughts and emotions and impulses and urges emanate. That's the paradigm I believed in, too, until I kept encountering clients who taught me otherwise. Because the mono-mind view is so ubiquitous and assumed in our culture, we never really question the truth of it. I want to help you take a look—a second look—at who you really are. I'm going to invite you to try on this different paradigm of multiplicity that IFS espouses and consider the possibility that you and everybody else is a multiple personality. And that is a good thing.

I'm not suggesting that you have Multiple Personality Disorder (now called Dissociative Identity Disorder), but I do think that people with that diagnosis are not so different from everybody else. What are called *alters* in those people are the same as what I call *parts* in IFS, and they exist in all of us. The only difference is that people with Dissociative Identity Disorder suffered horrible abuse and their system of parts got blown apart more than most, so each part stands out in bolder relief and is more polarized and disconnected from the others.

In other words, all of us are born with many sub-minds that are constantly interacting inside of us. This is in general what we call *thinking*, because the parts are talking to each other and to you constantly about things you have to do or debating the best course of action, and so on. Remembering a time when you faced a dilemma, it's likely you heard one part saying, "Go for it!" and another saying, "Don't you dare!" Because we just consider that to be a matter of having conflicted thoughts, we don't pay attention to the inner players behind the debate. IFS helps you not only start to pay attention to them, but also become the active internal leader that your system of parts needs.

While it may sound creepy or crazy at first to think of yourself as a multiple personality, I hope to convince you that it's actually quite empowering. It's only disturbing because multiplicity has been pathologized in our culture. A person with separate autonomous personalities is viewed as sick or damaged, and the existence of their alters is considered simply the product of trauma—the fragmentation of their previously unitary mind. From the mono-mind point of view, our natural condition is a unitary mind. Unless, of course, trauma comes along and shatters it into pieces, like shards of a vase.

The mono-mind paradigm has caused us to fear our parts and view them as pathological. In our attempts to control what we consider to be disturbing thoughts and emotions, we just end up fighting, ignoring, disciplining, hiding, or feeling ashamed of those impulses that keep us from doing what we want to do in our lives. And then we shame ourselves for not being able to control them. In other words, we hate what gets in our way.

This approach makes sense if you view these inner obstacles as merely irrational thoughts or extreme emotions that come from your unitary mind. If you fear giving a presentation, for example, you might try to use willpower to override the fear or correct it with rational thoughts. If the fear persists, you might escalate your attempts to control by criticizing yourself for being a coward, numbing yourself into oblivion, or meditating to climb above it. And when none of those approaches work, you wind up adapting your life to the fear—avoiding situations where you have to speak in public, feeling like a failure, and wondering what's wrong with you. To make matters worse, you go to a therapist who gives you a diagnosis for your one, troubled mind.

The diagnosis makes you feel defective, your self-esteem drops, and your feelings of shame lead you to attempt to hide any flaws and present a perfect image to the world. Or maybe you just withdraw from relationships for fear that people will see behind your mask and will judge you for it. You identify with your weaknesses, assuming that who you really are is defective and that if other people saw the real you, they'd be repulsed.

> "When people asked me if I was ready for my life to change, I don't think I really understood what they meant. It wasn't just that strangers would know who I was. It was this *other* thing that started to happen to me: when I looked in their eyes, sometimes, there was a little voice in my head wondering, *Would you still be so excited to meet me if you really knew who I was? If you knew all the things I have done? If you could see all my parts?*"
>
> *Queer Eye* star Jonathan Van Ness[1]

A Brief History

The mono-mind perspective, in combination with scientific and religious theories about how primitive human impulses are, created this backdrop of inner polarizations. One telling example comes from the influential Christian theologian John Calvin: "For our nature is not only utterly devoid of goodness, but so prolific in all kinds of evil, that it can never be idle . . . The whole man, from the crown of the head to the sole of the foot, is so deluged, as it were, that no part remains exempt from sin, and, therefore, everything which proceeds from him is imputed as sin."[2] This is known as the doctrine of *total depravity*, which insists that only through the grace of God can we escape our fate of eternal damnation. Mainstream Protestantism and Evangelicalism have carried some version of this doctrine for several hundred years, and the cultural impact has been widespread. With "Original Sin," Catholicism has its own version.

We can't blame this sort of thinking solely on religion, however. Generations of philosophers and politicians have asserted that primal impulses lurk just beneath the civilized veneer we present to the world. While Freud contributed important insights regarding the psyche, many of which are compatible with IFS, his drive theory was highly influential and pessimistic about human nature. It asserted that beneath the mind's surface lies selfish, aggressive, and pleasure-seeking instinctual forces that unconsciously organize our lives. Dutch historian Rutger Bregman summarizes these underlying assumptions about human nature here: "The doctrine that humans are innately selfish has a hallowed tradition in the Western canon. Great thinkers like Thucydides, Augustine, Machiavelli, Hobbes, Luther, Calvin, Burke, Bentham, Nietzsche, Freud, and America's Founding Fathers each had their own version of the veneer theory of civilization."[3]

Willpower and Shame

The emphasis on willpower and self-control permeates American culture. We think we should be able to discipline our primitive, impulsive, sinful minds through willpower. Countless self-help books tell us it's all a matter of boosting our ability to control ourselves and develop more discipline. The concept of willpower, too, has historical roots—namely in the Victorian Era with its Christian emphasis on resisting evil impulses. The idea of taking responsibility for oneself and not making excuses is as American as apple pie.

Sadly, our worship of willpower has been used by politicians and pundits to justify increasing levels of income disparity. We're taught that people are poor because they lack self-control and that rich people are wealthy because they have it, despite research to the contrary. Studies show, for example, that lower-income people become empowered and productive once they are given enough money to cover their basic survival needs.[4] However, the very real fact—especially considering the economic effects of the current pandemic—is that the rug could be pulled out from under most of us at any moment, and that threat keeps the survivalist parts of us humming.

Because this willpower ethic has become internalized, we learn at an early age to shame and manhandle our unruly parts. We simply wrestle them into submission. One part is recruited by this cultural imperative to become our inner drill sergeant and often becomes that nasty inner critic we love to hate. This is the voice that tries to shame us or attempts to outright get rid of parts of us that seem shame-worthy (the ones that give us nasty thoughts about people, for example, or keep us addicted to substances).

We often find that the harder we try to get rid of emotions and thoughts, the stronger they become.

We often find that the harder we try to get rid of emotions and thoughts, the stronger they become. This is because parts, like people, fight back against being shamed or exiled. And if we do succeed in dominating them with punitive self-discipline, we then become tyrannized by the rigid, controlling inner drill sergeant. We might be disciplined, but we're not much fun. And because the exiled (bingeing, raging, hypersexual, etc.) parts will seize any momentary weakness to break out again and take over, we have to constantly be on guard against any people or situations that might trigger those parts.

Jonathan Van Ness tried and failed at drug rehab several times. "Growing up around so much 12-Step, and seeing so much abstinence preached in rehab and in church, I started to take on an idea that healing had to be all or nothing, which has really not been my truth. I was trying to untangle sexual abuse, drug abuse, and PTSD, and it was something that for me wasn't conducive to a never-ever-smoking-weed-again approach. . . . I don't believe that once an addict, always an addict. I don't believe that addiction is a disease that warrants a life sentence. . . . If you ever mess up or can't string a couple of months together without a slipup, you're not ruined."[5]

There are 12-Step approaches that aren't so locked in to the rigid beliefs that Van Ness encountered, and the groups can be a wonderful context for people to be vulnerable and receive support. Also, the 12-Step admonition to give everything up to a higher power can often help inner drill instructors lighten up or even surrender. The larger point I want to make here is that any approach that increases your inner drill sergeant's impulse to shame you into behaving (and make you feel like a failure if you can't) will do no better in internal families than it does in external ones in which parents adopt shaming tactics to control their children.

Don't think that this critique of willpower reveals that there's no room for inner discipline in IFS. Like children in external families, we each have parts that want things that aren't good for them or for the rest of the system. The difference here is that the Self says no to impulsive parts firmly but from a place of love and patience, in just the same way an ideal parent would. Additionally, in IFS, when parts do take over, we don't shame them. Instead, we get curious and use the part's impulse as a trailhead to find what is driving it that needs to be healed.

Parts Aren't Obstacles

The mono-mind paradigm can easily lead us to fear or hate ourselves because we believe we have only one mind (full of primitive or sinful aspects) that we can't control. We get tied up in knots as we desperately try to, and we generate brutal inner critics who attack us for our failings. As Van Ness notes, "I spent so much time pushing little Jack aside. Instead of nurturing him I tore him to pieces. . . . Learning to parent yourself, with soothing compassionate love . . . that's the key to being fulfilled."[6]

Since most psychotherapies and spiritual practices subscribe to this mono-mind view, their solutions often reinforce this approach by suggesting we should correct irrational beliefs or meditate them away, because those beliefs are seen as obstacles emanating from our one mind. Many approaches to meditation, for example, view thoughts as pests and the ego as a hindrance or annoyance, and practitioners are given instructions to either ignore or transcend them.

In some Hindu traditions, the ego is viewed as working for the god Maya, whose goal is to keep us striving for material things or hedonistic pleasures. She is considered the enemy—a temptress much like the Christian Satan—who keeps us attached to the external world of illusion.

Buddhist teachings use the term *monkey mind* to describe how our thoughts jump around in our consciousness like an agitated monkey. As

Ralph De La Rosa notes in *The Monkey Is the Messenger*, "Is it any wonder that the monkey mind is the scourge of meditators across the globe? For those trying to find respite in contemplative practice, thoughts are often regarded as an irritating nuisance, a primitive agitator sneaking in through the side door. . . . In meditation circles, some unintended consequences of the monkey metaphor prevail: that the thinking mind is a dirty, primitive, lower life form of no real value to us; it's just a bunch of garbage on repeat."[7]

De La Rosa is one of a number of recent authors who challenge the common practice in spirituality of vilifying the ego. Another is psychotherapist Matt Licata, who writes,

> 'The ego' is often spoken about as if it is some sort of self-existing thing that at times takes us over—some nasty, super unspiritual, ignorant little person living inside—and causes us to act in really unevolved ways creating unending messes in our lives and getting in the way of our progress on the path. It is something to be horribly ashamed of and the more spiritual we are the more we will strive to 'get rid of it,' transcend it, or enter into imaginary spiritual wars with it. If we look carefully, we may see that if the ego is anything, it is likely those very voices that are yelling at us to get rid of it.[8]

The collection of parts that these traditions call the ego are protectors who are simply trying to keep us safe and are reacting to and containing other parts that carry emotions and memories from past traumas that we have locked away inside.

Later we'll look more closely at some of the ways people practice spiritual bypassing—a phrase coined by John Welwood in the 1980s. Jeff Brown explores the phenomenon in depth in his film *Karmageddon*: "After my childhood, I needed the kinds of spirituality that would keep me from allowing the pain to surface. . . . I was confusing self-avoidance with enlightenment."[9] In fact, one central message in the canonical story of the Buddha's awakening is that thoughts and desires are the primary obstacles to enlightenment. As he sat in meditation beneath the Bodhi Tree, the Buddha was assaulted by a series of impulses and urges—lust, desire, fulfillment, regret, fear, insecurity, and so on—and it was only by ignoring or resisting them that he was able to attain enlightenment.

That being said, the ubiquitous, Buddhist-derived practices of mindfulness are a step in the right direction. They enable the practitioner to observe thoughts and emotions from a distance and from a place of acceptance rather than fighting or ignoring them. For me, that's a good first step. Mindfulness is not always pleasant, however. Researchers who interviewed experienced meditators found that substantial percentages of them had disturbing episodes that sometimes were long-lasting. The most common of those included emotions like fear, anxiety, paranoia, detachment, and reliving traumatic memories.[10] From the IFS point of view, the quieting of the mind associated with mindfulness happens when the parts of us usually running our lives (our egos) relax, which then allows parts we have tried to bury (exiles) to ascend, bringing with them the emotions, beliefs, and memories they carry (burdens) that got them locked away in the first place. Most of the mindfulness approaches I'm familiar with subscribe to the mono-mind paradigm and, consequently, view such episodes as the temporary emergence of troubling thoughts and emotions rather than as hurting parts that need to be listened to and loved. Why would you want to converse with thoughts and emotions? They can't talk back, can they? Well, it turns out that they can. In fact, they have a lot of important things to tell us.

How I Came to Learn About Parts

I started out like everybody else thinking the mind is unitary and I trained as a family therapist for years (in fact, I have a PhD in the field). As family therapists, we didn't pay much attention to the mind at all. We thought the therapists who mucked around in that inner world were wasting their time, because we could change all that simply by changing external relationships.

The only problem was the approach didn't work. I did an outcome study with bulimic clients and discovered with alarm that they kept binging and purging, not realizing they'd been cured. When I asked them why, they started talking about these different parts of them. And they talked about these parts as if they had a lot of autonomy—as if they could take over and make them do things they didn't want to do. At first, I was scared that I was looking at an outbreak of Multiple Personality Disorder, but then I started listening inside myself and I was shocked to find that I had parts too. In fact, some of mine were fairly extreme.

So I started getting curious. I asked the clients to describe their parts, which they were able to do in great detail. Not only that, but they depicted how these parts interacted with each other and had relationships. Some fought, some formed alliances, and some protected others. Over time, it dawned on me that I was learning about a kind of inner system, not unlike the "external" families I was working with. Hence the name: Internal Family Systems.

For example, clients would talk about an inner critic who, when they made a mistake, attacked them mercilessly. That attack would trigger a part that felt totally bereft, lonely, empty, and worthless. Experiencing that worthless part was so distressing that almost to the rescue would come the binge that would take clients out of their body and turn them into an unfeeling eating machine. Then the critic would attack them for the binge, which retriggered the worthlessness, and they found themselves caught in these terrible circles for days on end.

At first, I tried to get clients to relate to these parts in a way that would shut them out or get them to stop. For example, I suggested ignoring the critical part or arguing with it. This approach just made things worse, but I didn't know what else to do than encourage them to fight harder to win their inner battles.

I had one client who had a part that made her cut her wrists. Well, I couldn't stand for that. My client and I badgered the part in one session for a couple of hours until it agreed not to cut her wrists anymore. I left that session feeling drained, but satisfied that we had won the battle.

I opened the door to our next session and my client had a big gash across her face. I collapsed emotionally at that point and spontaneously said, "I give up, I can't beat you at this," and the part shifted, too, and said, "I don't really want to beat you." That was a turning point in the history of this work, because I moved out of that controlling place and took on a more curious approach: "Why do you do this to her?" The part proceeded to talk about how it had needed to get my client out of her body when she was being abused and control the rage that would only result in more abuse. I shifted again and conveyed an appreciation for the heroic role it played in her life. The part broke into tears. Everyone had demonized it and tried to get rid of it. This was the first time it had the chance to tell its story.

I told the part that it made total sense that it had to do that to save the woman's life in the past, but why did it still have to cut her now? It spoke of having to protect other highly vulnerable parts of her and it had to control the rage that was still there. As it talked about all of that, it became clear to me that the cutting part wasn't living in the present. It seemed frozen in those abuse scenes and believed that my client was still a child and in grave danger, even though she wasn't anymore.

It began to dawn on me that maybe these parts aren't what they seem. Maybe, like children in dysfunctional families, they are forced out of their natural, valuable states into roles that sometimes can be destructive but are, they think, necessary to protect the person or the system they are in. So I started trying to help my clients listen to their troublesome parts rather than fight them, and was astounded to find that their parts all had similar stories to tell of how they had to take on protective roles at some point in the person's past—often roles that they hated but felt were needed to save the client.

When I asked these protective parts what they'd rather do if they trusted they didn't have to protect, they often wanted to do something opposite of the role they were in. Inner critics wanted to become cheerleaders or sage advisors, extreme caretakers wanted to help set boundaries, rageful parts wanted to help with discerning who was safe. It seemed that not only were parts not what they seemed, but also they each had qualities and resources to bring to the client's life that were not available while they were tied up in the protective roles.

Now, several decades and thousands of clients later (and thousands of therapists doing IFS around the world), I can safely say that this is true of parts. They can become quite extreme and do a lot of damage in a person's life, but there aren't any that are inherently bad. Even the ones that make bulimics binge or anorexics starve or make people want to kill themselves or murder people, even those parts when approached from this mindful place—this respectful, open, curious place—will reveal the secret history of how they were forced into the role they're in and how they're stuck in that role, terrified that if they don't do it something dreadful will happen. And, that they're frozen in the past, during the traumatic times when they had to take on the role.

Let's pause here to explore the spiritual implications of this discovery. Basically, what I found is that love is the answer in the inner world, just as it is in the outer world. Listening to, embracing, and loving parts allows them to heal and transform as much as it does for people. In Buddhist terms, IFS helps people become bodhisat-tvas of their psyches in the sense of helping each inner sentient being (part) become enlightened through compassion and love. Or, through a Christian lens, through IFS people wind up doing in the inner world what Jesus did in the outer—they go to inner exiles and enemies with love, heal them, and bring them home, just as he did with the lepers, the poor, and the outcasts.

IFS helps people become bodhisattvas of their psyches.

The big conclusion here is that parts are not what they have been commonly thought to be. They're not cognitive adaptations or sinful impulses. Instead, parts are sacred, spiritual beings and they deserve to be treated as such.

Another theme we will be exploring in this book is how it's all parallel—how we relate in the inner world will be how we relate in the outer. If we can appreciate and have compassion for our parts, even for the ones we've considered to be enemies, we can do the same for people who resemble them. On the other hand, if we hate or disdain our parts, we'll do the same with anyone who reminds us of them.

Some discoveries I made about parts:
- Even the most destructive parts have protective intentions.
- Parts are often frozen in past traumas when their extreme roles were needed.
- When they trust it's safe to step out of their roles, they are highly valuable to the system.

Burdens

Here's another key discovery I stumbled on: parts carry extreme beliefs and emotions in or on their "bodies" that drive the way they feel and act.

The idea that parts have bodies that are separate and different from the person's body they are connected to may seem strange or preposterous at first. Let me interject here that I am simply reporting what I've learned over years of exploring this inner territory without judgment regarding the ontological reality of that data. If you ask your parts about their own bodies, I predict you'll get the same answers I'm covering here.

For a long time, I didn't know what to make of this discovery. Regardless, this is how parts describe themselves—that they have bodies and that their bodies contain emotions and beliefs that came into them and don't belong to them. Often, they can tell you the exact traumatic moment these emotions and beliefs came into or attached to them and they can tell you where they carry what seem to them to be these foreign objects in or on their bodies. "It's this tar on my arms" or "a fireball in my gut" or "a huge weight on my shoulders," for example. These foreign feelings or beliefs (sometimes described as energies) are what I call *burdens*. It turns out that burdens are powerful organizers of a part's experience and activity—almost in the same way that a virus organizes a computer.

It's important to note here that these burdens are the product of a person's direct experience—the sense of worthlessness that comes into a child when a parent abuses them; the terror that attaches to parts during a car accident; the belief that no one can be trusted that enters young parts when we are betrayed or abandoned as children. When we are young, we have little discernment regarding the validity of these emotions and beliefs and, consequently, they get lodged in the bodies of our young parts and become powerful (albeit unconscious) organizers of our lives thereafter. These we call *personal burdens*.

Some of the most powerful personal burdens are similar to what attachment theory pioneer John Bowlby called *internal working models*.[11] He saw them as maps you developed as a child of what to expect from your caretaker and the world in general, and then from subsequent close relationships. They also tell you things about your own level of goodness and how much you deserve love and support.

There is another class of burdens that are called *legacy burdens* because they did not come from your direct life experience. Instead, you inherited them from your parents, who got them from their parents, and so on. Or you absorbed them from your ethnic group or from the culture you currently live in. Legacy burdens can be equally if not more potent organizers of our lives, and because we've had them so long we marinate in them, so it's often harder to notice them than the personal burdens we took on from traumas. In this way, legacy burdens can be as prominent and unnoticed as water to a fish.

Parts Are Not Their Burdens

This distinction between parts and the burdens they carry is crucial because many of the world's problems are related to the error that most paradigms for understanding the mind make: to mistake the burden for the part that carries it.

It's common to believe that a person who gets high all the time is an addict who has an irresistible urge to use drugs. That belief leads to combatting that person's urge with opioid antagonists, with recovery programs that can have the effect of polarizing the addictive part, or with the willpower of the addict. If, on the other hand, you believe that the part that seeks drugs is protective and carries the burden of responsibility for keeping this person from severe emotional pain or even suicide, then you would treat the person very differently. You could instead help them get to know that part and honor it for its attempts to keep them going and negotiate permission to heal or change what it protects.

Then you would help the person heal by returning to the now liberated "addict" part and help it unburden all its fear and responsibility. *Unburdening* is another aspect of IFS that seems spiritual, because as soon as the burdens leave parts' bodies, parts immediately transform into their original, valuable states. It's as if a curse was lifted from an inner Sleeping Beauty, or ogre, or addict. The newly unburdened part almost universally says it feels much lighter and wants to play or rest, after which it finds a new role. The former addict part now wants to help you connect with people. The hypervigilant part becomes an advisor

It's as if each part is like a person with a true purpose.

on boundaries. The critic becomes an inner cheerleader, and so on. In other words, it's as if each part is like a person with a true purpose.

No Bad Parts

If the title of the book didn't trigger this question for you, I'll ask it directly now: What are we to do with parts that have committed terrible violence? What about those that have murdered or sexually abused people? Or parts that are determined to kill their person? How in the world can these be good parts in bad roles?

As I did IFS with clients it became increasingly clear that the burdens that drove their parts were rooted in early traumas, so in the late 1980s and early 1990s I came to specialize in the treatment of those who had suffered complex trauma and carried serious diagnoses like borderline personality disorder, chronic depression, and eating disorders. I also became interested in understanding and treating perpetrators of abuse because it became clear that healing one of them could potentially save many future victims in turn.

For seven years I consulted to Onarga Academy, a treatment center in Illinois for sex offenders. I had the opportunity to help those clients listen to the parts of them that had molested children, and over and over I heard the same story: While the offender was being abused as a child, one of their protector parts became desperate to protect them and took on the rageful or sexually violent energy of their perpetrator and used that energy to protect themself from that abuser. From that point on, however, this protector part continued to carry that burden of the perpetrator's hatred and desire to dominate and punish vulnerability. The part also was frozen in time during the abuse.

Thus, the kick in molesting a child came from being able to hurt and have power over someone weak and innocent. These perpetrator parts would do the same thing in their psyches to their own vulnerable, childlike parts. This process—in which protectors in one generation take on the perpetrator burdens of their parents while they were being abused by those parents—is one way that legacy burdens are transferred.

As we healed their parts stuck in early abuse, their perpetrator parts unloaded their parents' violent or sexual energies and, like other parts, quickly transformed and took on valuable roles. During this period, I had the opportunity to work with other kinds of perpetrators (including murderers) with similar findings. I remembered that famous Will Rodgers saying, "I never met a man I didn't like," and I realized that I could say that about parts. I ultimately liked all of them—even the ones that had done heinous things.

Now, decades later, I've worked with countless clients (as have other IFS therapists around the world) and I believe it is safe to say that there are no bad parts. Spiritual traditions encourage us to have compassion for everyone. This aspect of IFS actually helps make that possible. IFS operates from the radically different assumption that each part—no matter how demonic seeming—has a secret, painful history to share of how it was forced into its role and came to carry burdens it doesn't like that continue to drive it. This also implies clear steps for helping these parts and the people they are in to heal and change. It brings hope to the hopeless.

The Self

In those early days of helping my clients listen to and form better relationships with their parts, I tried out a technique from Gestalt therapy involving multiple chairs. Basically, a client sits in one chair and talks to an empty chair across from them, and for IFS I had them imagine that the part they were talking to was in that empty chair. And because the parts got to speak, too, there was a lot of hopping back and forth, and to make it all work I ended up with an office full of chairs. I watched clients shift around the room, being their different parts, and it actually helped me learn a lot about the patterns among the parts. Then one insightful client suggested that moving from chair to chair might be unnecessary and that they could do the same work by just sitting in one seat. That method went fine for that particular client, and when I tried it out with others, they found they could do it that way too.

My main goal was to help my clients form better relationships with their parts. Some of the patterns I kept seeing with individuals were similar to what

I witnessed as a family therapist. For example, a bulimic kid would be speaking with their critical part and all of a sudden, they'd become angry at the critic and yell at it. In family therapy, let's say this client is a girl talking to her critical mother and she gets mad and shouts at her mother. In such cases, we're taught to look around the room and see if anyone is covertly siding with the girl against the mother—for example, the girl's father is signaling to her that he disagrees with the mother too. This is when I'd ask the father to step back out of the girl's line of vision, she'd slowly calm down, and things would go better with her conversation with her mother.

So I started using this "step back" technique with individuals. I'd have them ask other parts to step aside so that pairs of parts could really dig in and listen to each other. For example, I might say, "Could you find the one who's angry at the target part [in this case the critic] and just ask it to step back for a little while?" To my amazement, most clients said, "Okay, it did" without much hesitation, and when the part was off to the side like that, my clients would shift into an entirely different state. And then other parts would step in (a fearful part, for example) and the more of them that stepped back to allow the client to speak, the more mindful and curious the client would become. The simple act of getting these other parts to open more space inside seemed to release someone who had curiosity but who was also calm and confident relative to the critic.

The Self is in everybody.

When my clients were in that place, the dialogue would go well. The critic would drop its guard and tell its secret history and the client would have compassion for it and we would learn about what it protected, and so on. Client after client, the same mindfully curious, calm, confident, and often even compassionate part would pop up out of the blue and that part seemed to know how to relate internally in a healing way. And when they were in that state, I'd ask clients, "Now, what part of you is that?" and they'd say, "That's not a part like these others, that's more myself" or "That's more my core" or "That's who I really am."

That's the part that I call the Self. And after thousands of hours doing this work, I can say with certainty that the Self is in everybody. Furthermore, the Self cannot be damaged, the Self doesn't have to develop, and the Self possesses its own wisdom about how to heal internal as well as external relationships.

For me, this is the most significant discovery that I stumbled onto. This is what changes everything. The Self is just beneath the surface of our protective parts, such that when they open space for it, it comes forward spontaneously, often quite suddenly, and universally.

Your Turn

So that's my introduction to IFS. It makes a certain amount of conceptual sense to many people initially, but until you've actually experienced it, it's hard to fully get what I'm talking about. So now it's your turn. I'm going to invite you to try an exercise designed to give you a start on getting to know yourself in this different way.

Exercise: Getting to Know a Protector

Take a second and get comfortable. Set up like you would if you were going to meditate. If it helps you to take deep breaths, then do that.

Now I invite you to do a scan of your body and your mind, noting in particular any thoughts, emotions, sensations, or impulses that stand out. So far, it's not unlike mindfulness practice, where you're just noticing what's there and separating from it a little bit.

As you do that, see if one of those emotions, thoughts, sensations, or impulses is calling to you—seems to want your attention. If so, then try to focus on it exclusively for a minute and see if you can notice where it seems to be located in your body or around your body.

As you notice it, notice how *you* feel toward it. By that I mean, do you dislike it? Does it annoy you? Are you afraid of it? Do you want to get rid of it? Do you depend on it? So we're just noticing that you have a relationship with this thought, emotion, sensation, or impulse. If you feel anything besides a kind of openness or curiosity toward it, then ask the parts of you that might not like it or are afraid of it or have any other extreme feeling about it to just relax inside and give you a little space to get to know it without an attitude.

If you can't get to that curious place, that's okay. You could spend the time talking to the parts of you that don't want to relax about their fears about letting you actually interact with the target emotion, thought, sensation, or impulse.

But if you can get into that mindfully curious place relative to the target, then it is safe to begin to interact with it. That might feel a bit odd to you at this point, but just give it a try. And by that, I mean as you focus on this emotion or impulse or thought or sensation and you notice it in this place in your body, ask it if there's something it wants you to know and then wait for an answer. Don't think of the answer, so any thinking parts can relax too. Just wait silently with your focus on that place in your body until an answer comes and if nothing comes, that's okay too.

If you get an answer, then as a follow-up you can ask what it's afraid would happen if it didn't do this inside of you. What's it afraid would happen if it didn't do what it does? And if it answers that question, then you probably learned something about how it's trying to protect you. If that's true, then see if it's possible to extend some appreciation to it for at least trying to keep you safe and see how it reacts to your appreciation. Then ask this part of you what it needs from you in the future.

When the time feels right, shift your focus back to the outside world and notice more of your surroundings, but also thank your parts for whatever they allowed you to do and let them know that this isn't their last chance to have a conversation with you, because you plan to get to know them even more.

I hope you were able to follow me in that journey and that you got some information. Sometimes what you learn can be quite surprising. And for me, these emotions, sensations, thoughts, impulses, and other things are emanations from parts—they are what we call *trailheads*. This is because when you focus on one, it's as if you are starting out on a trail that will lead you to the part from which that thought, emotion, impulse, or sensation emanates. And, as you get to know that part, you will learn that it isn't just that thought, sensation, impulse, or emotion. Indeed, it will let you know that it has a whole range of feelings and thoughts, and it can tell you about the role it is in and why it does what it does. Then it will feel seen by you and you can honor it.

That's what I started to do with my clients in the early 1980s and an entirely new world opened up in the process of doing that. It reminded me of high school biology class when we looked in the microscope at a drop of pond water and were shocked to see all kinds of little paramecia, protozoa, and amoebas scurrying around in it. When we simply turn our attention inside, we find that what we thought were random thoughts and emotions comprise a buzzing inner community that has been interacting behind the scenes throughout our lives.

In this exercise you may have noticed that by simply focusing on one of your parts, you were separating (*unblending*) from it. In other words, suddenly there was a *you* who was observing and an *it* that was being observed. As I said in the introduction, you'll find this type of separation in mindfulness practices, and it's a great first step. Then you took the next step when you explored how you feel about it and noticed what other parts feel about it. When you feel angry or afraid of it, that wouldn't be the Self, but other parts that are still blended with the Self.

If you were able to get those parts to step back and open space, it's likely you felt a shift into more mindfulness. From my point of view, your Self was being accessed through that unblending. The simple act of getting other parts to open space brings the Self forward, and a lot of meditation works by simply getting you to that more spacious, emptier mind and enabling you to feel the sense of calm well-being that fills that space.

In this process you turn toward what you're observing and begin a new relationship with it.

But instead of simply observing what most traditions think of as the ego or as mere ephemeral thoughts and emotions, in this process you turn toward what you're observing and begin a new relationship with it, one that involves a lot of curiosity. Ideally, you can continue to deepen the relationship, and parts really appreciate it when you do that. Usually, they've been operating by themselves in there without any adult supervision, and most of them are pretty young. When you finally turn around and give them some attention, it's like you're a parent who's been somewhat neglectful, but who's finally becoming more nurturing and interested in your children.

Exercise: Mapping Your Parts

Now I'm going to invite you to get to know a cluster of parts that have relationships with each other. To do that you'll need a pad of paper and a pencil or pen. Again, focus inside and think of another part—not the one you just worked with, but a different one that you'd like to start with this time. The trailhead could be any emotion, thought, belief, impulse, or sensation.

As you focus on this new part, find it in your body or on your body. And now, just stay focused on it until you get enough of a sense of it that you could represent it on the page in front of you. It doesn't have to be high art—any kind of image is good. It could even be a scribble. Just find a way to represent that part of you on a blank page. Stay focused on the part until you know how to represent it and then draw it.

After you've put that first part on the page, focus again on that same one in the same place in your body and just stay focused on it until you notice some kind of a shift and another trailhead—another part—emerges. And when that happens, focus on that second one, find it in your body, and stay with it until you can represent it on the page also.

After you've drawn that second one, go back to it again and stay with it until you notice yet another shift and another trailhead emerges. And then shift your focus to this new one, find it in your body, and stay with it until you can represent it on the page. Then, once again we'll go back to that third one, focus on it in that place in your body, and just stay present to that until still another one comes forward. And then shift to that one, find it in your body, and stay with it until you can represent it.

You can repeat this process until you have a sense that you have mapped out one complete system inside you. When you feel you've done that, shift your focus back outside to your surroundings.

It's likely that what you found is one *clove of the garlic*, as we call it in IFS. You might be familiar with the onion analogy used in psychotherapy—you peel your layers off and you get to this core and then you heal that and you're done. Well, in IFS it's more like a garlic bulb. You have all these different cloves, each of which has a handful of different parts inside that are related to each other, and maybe are all stuck in one place in the past. As you work with one clove, you'll feel relief from the burdens it contained, but you may not have touched other cloves that revolved around other traumas. So this mapping exercise is designed to bring forth one of your cloves—one subsystem within you. Feel free to continue and map out other cloves.

Now I'd like you to hold your page a little bit away from you, so extend your arms with your pad of paper all the way out and look at these four or five parts you've represented with a little perspective. How do the parts relate to each other? Do some protect others? Do some fight with each other? Is there some kind of alliance in there? As you start to form some answers, make a note on your drawing to represent them.

Now I want you to look at the parts again and explore how you feel toward each of them. When you're done with that, think about what this system needs from you. Finally, take a second to focus inside again and just thank these parts for revealing themselves to you and let them know again that this isn't the last time you'll be talking to them. Then shift your focus back outside again.

I recommend this exercise for many contexts. For example, if you have a pressing issue in your life, go inside and map it out and some of the answers will come to you—either about what decision to make or about what parts are making it so difficult. Mapping your parts is another way to separate from them, as well, because often we're quite blended with more than one.

CHAPTER TWO

Why Parts Blend

In IFS, we use the term *blended* to describe the phenomenon in which a part merges its perspective, emotion, beliefs, and impulses with your Self. When that happens, the qualities of your Self are obscured and seem to be replaced by those of the part. You might feel overwhelmed with fear, anger, or apathy. You might dissociate or become confused or have cravings. In other words, at least temporarily you become the part that has blended with you. You are the fearful young girl or the pouting little boy you once were.

Why do parts blend? Protective parts blend because they believe they have to manage situations in your life. They don't trust your Self to do it. For example, if your father hit you as a child and you weren't able to stop him, your parts lost trust in your Self's ability to protect the system and, instead, came to believe they have to do it. To make the parallel to external families, they become parentified inner children. That is, they carry the responsibility for protecting you despite the fact that, like external parentified children, they are not equipped to do so.

Parts often become extreme in their protective efforts and take over your system by blending. Some make you hypervigilant, others get you to overreact angrily to perceived slights, others make you somewhat dissociative all the time or cause you to fully dissociate in the face of perceived threats. Some become the inner critics as they try to motivate you to look or perform better or try to shame you into not taking risks. Others make you take care of everyone around you and neglect yourself.

The list of common protector roles in traumatized systems could go on and on. The point here is that these symptoms and patterns are the activities of young, stressed-out parts that are often frozen in time during earlier traumas and believe that you are still quite young and powerless. They often believe that they must blend the way they do or something dreadful will happen (often, that you will die). Given where they are stuck in the past, it makes sense that they would believe this.

Some of us are blended with some parts most of the time and we are so used to it that we don't even think the beliefs we consequently hold are extreme. We just have a background sense that we are a fraud, that we shouldn't fully trust anyone, or that we have to work constantly to avoid becoming impoverished. We may not even be consciously aware of such beliefs—yet those burdens govern our lives and are never examined or questioned.

Other parts only blend when they are triggered—someone rejects us, and suddenly we are awash in shame; a driver cuts us off, and we're flooded with rage; we have to prepare for a presentation, and we have a panic attack.

Like the sun, the Self can be temporarily obscured, but it never disappears.

We know that they're overreactions, but we have no real idea as to why we get so upset. And because we never ask inside, we just go around thinking of ourselves as touchy, angry, or anxious people.

It's important to remember that regardless of how blended we are, the Self is still in there—it never goes away. In ancient times, when there was a solar eclipse and it suddenly got dark because the moon blocked the sun, people would panic, believing the sun had disappeared. Like the sun, the Self can be temporarily obscured, but it never disappears. When the moon passes by or clouds dissipate, the sun shines as brightly as ever. Similarly, when parts unblend, the Self's nourishing energy is readily available again and the parts are comforted to sense the presence of such a strong, loving inner leader.

Blended parts give us the projections, transferences, and other twisted views that are the bread and butter of psychotherapy. The Self's view is unfiltered by those distortions. When we're in Self, we see the pain that drives our enemies rather than only seeing their protective parts.

Your protectors only see the protectors of others.

Your protectors only see the protectors of others. The clarity of Self gives you a kind of X-ray vision, so you see behind the other person's protectors to their vulnerability, and in turn your heart opens to them.

Self also senses the Self in everyone and, consequently, has a deep sense of connectedness, as well as a strong desire to connect to the Self of others. This sense of connectedness has a spiritual element to it that we'll explore later in this book—we feel connected to Spirit, the Tao, God, Brahman, to the Big Self. We feel that because we *are* connected to it.

When we blend with burdened parts, we lose all sense of this connectedness and feel separate from one another and from spirit—alone and lonely. Here is another parallel between inner and outer systems. After they are burdened, our parts feel lonely and disconnected from one another and from our Self. They don't realize they are all affected by what happens to each other and are loved by Self. Neither do we.

Thus, finding blended parts and helping them trust that it's safe to unblend is a crucial part of IFS. As you might have discovered in the mapping exercise, the simple act of noticing parts and representing them on a page often creates enough separation from them (enough unblending) that you can have a different perspective on them. Like the view of a city from thirty thousand feet, you can see more clearly the roles they take on and how they operate as a system. Once you're out of the trees, you can see the forest.

Not only can you see them better, it is easier to care about each of them when you are above, rather than in the middle of, their crossfires. When you unblend enough from the parts that hate your fear, for example, you suddenly see that it's not a bundle of irrational neuroses but a frightened little child-like part who needs to be comforted. You have compassion for the little guy and want to hold rather than scold him. You find that holding parts actually works—you're no longer plagued by fear.

Many spiritual traditions stress the importance of loving, or at least having compassion for, yourself. IFS tells you precisely how to do that. For example, Kristin Neff and Chris Germer have brought a large and wonderful movement to the public called Mindful Self-Compassion, based on some Buddhist practices that are quite compatible with IFS. IFS makes such practices a little more concrete by helping you extend care and nurturance to specific parts that are suffering or are former enemies, and you can notice how they react.

Also, whereas some traditions teach that you have to build up the muscle of compassion with specific practices, with IFS, the Self is already buff with compassion. It merely needs to be released, not strengthened. Daily practices can be useful in helping parts trust that it is safe to release compassion, and that can be expedited by getting to know and addressing their fears about doing so.

In fact, most meditations can be seen as unblending practices. Whether you mindfully separate from thoughts and emotions by noticing them from a place of calm acceptance or by repeating a mantra that puts them to sleep, you are accessing the Self. As those meditations help you have more calm, confidence, clarity, compassion, courage, creativity, curiosity, and connectedness in your life (more on these eight Cs in a little bit), your parts come to trust your Self more to lead inside and out. IFS offers a particular approach to meditation that you can experience in the next exercise.

Exercise: Unblending and Embodying

This is a brief meditation that I do a version of each day, as do many people who follow the IFS path. I encourage you to try it out as a daily practice.

Get comfortable and, if it helps, take deep breaths. Then start by focusing on and checking in with whatever parts you are actively working with. To do that, see if you can find each of them in or around your body and get curious about how they're doing. That is, ask each if there's anything it wants you to know or if it needs anything—like you might with a child that's in your care.

As you're getting to know it, at some point help it get to know you better—the you that's with it now—since most of the time these parts don't really know you. Instead, they've been interacting with other parts in there and they often believe that you are still a young child.

Often this is their first encounter with you—the you who's curious about them and cares about them. So let them know who you are, even how old you are, since they often think you're much younger. Let them know that they're not alone anymore and see how they react. You can ask, if you like, how old they thought you were. You can even ask them to turn around and look at you.

After you've checked in with the parts you've begun working with, you can open space and invite any other parts that need attention to come forward and just wait and see what trailheads—thoughts, emotions, sensations, impulses—emerge. In a similar way, get to know these new ones and help them get to know you.

This next piece is optional and may or may not happen. Revisit each of them one at a time and invite them to relax and open space inside, so you can be more in your body. If a part's willing to do that, you'll notice a palpable shift in your body or your mind toward more spaciousness and peace in that place where the part seems to reside. If that doesn't happen, don't despair, as they may not know you well enough yet to trust that it's safe to do that, and that's fine.

If they do separate, notice that more embodied, spacious sense of who you are and the qualities you feel when you're in that place. What's it like in your body and mind now? Notice that spaciousness, the sense of well-being and enoughness—that you are enough. Also notice the feeling like there's nothing to do right now and everything is okay. Some people spontaneously feel a vibrating energy running through their body, making their fingers and toes tingle. This is what some people call chi or kundalini or prana, but in IFS we call it Self energy.

I'm inviting you to get a felt sense of what it's like for you, your Self, to be more embodied. If you can become somatically familiar with this state, then you can notice when you're there and when you're not as you go through your day. Any departures from that state are usually due to the activity of parts that have blended to some degree and are giving you distracting thoughts, blocking the flow of energy, closing your heart, making you feel pressure in different places, et cetera. You can notice those activities and then reassure the parts doing them that they don't have to—that it's safe to unblend, at least for the duration of the meditation. Afterward they can jump back to attention if they really want to. I have found, however, that through this practice, parts gradually increase their trust that it is safe and beneficial to let the Self embody. They also trust that the Self is remembering and checking on them—that it's being a good inner parent. All of this Self-leadership helps them step out of their parentified roles and consider unburdening.

In the next minute or so, I invite you to shift your focus back outside. Before you come back, though, thank your parts either for letting you embody more or, if they didn't, for letting you know they were too afraid to do so just yet. Then come on back when it feels right.

The Four Basic Goals of IFS

1. Liberate parts from the roles they've been forced into, so they can be who they're designed to be.

2. Restore trust in the Self and Self-leadership.

3. Reharmonize the inner system.

4. Become more Self-led in your interactions with the world.

This kind of unblending doesn't have to be limited to twenty-minute sessions. It can become a life practice. As I go through my day, I notice how much I'm in my body—how much of my Self is present. I'll check my heart to see how open it is, feel whether my mind is also open or if I have a strong agenda or pressured thoughts, gauge the resonance of my voice when I talk, feel whether or not that vibrating Self energy is flowing, examine whether there is the physical tension in my forehead or weight on my shoulders (which is where my managers hang out), et cetera. These are some of my markers, and I encourage you to find your own.

After practicing many years, I can check those markers quickly and then ask any activated parts to relax, separate, and trust me to embody. Because my parts trust me now, most of the time I'll quickly notice changes in all those qualities and places in my body. There are a few circumstances where that is still a challenge, but that simply means that I still need to heal some parts that get triggered by those situations. When you can be present with your parts in the inner world this way, you can lead more of your life in the outer world from this place.

In this meditation, I had you tell your parts how old you really are. When I have people ask that question (i.e., "How old do you think I am?"), maybe 70 percent of the time the answer is in single digits. Often the number that comes back to you is the age you were when the part was forced out of its valuable state and into the role that it's in now. It's like once the part took on that role, it focused on the outside world and never looked back at you—it didn't notice that you grew. So, many parts believe they are still protecting you as a young child. In many cases, how old you are now is a big revelation to these parts—many don't believe it at first.

The goal of this updating process is for your parts to realize that they aren't the Lone Rangers they thought they were in there. Instead, as they come to trust you—your Self—as the inner leader, they are greatly relieved and can become who they are designed to be. They may grow a bit older or younger or stay the same age, but universally they transform into valuable roles.

More About Parts

Before we go any deeper into this work, I want to make sure I'm clear about what I'm calling parts. As I discussed earlier, parts are typically mistaken for the extreme roles they are in. As a consequence, we just end up fighting, shunning, or disparaging them.

There is a parallel with other people here. After being traumatized or repeatedly humiliated, people often behave in extreme ways—they have addictions, rage, or panic attacks, become narcissistic or obsessed. Our culture and psychiatric establishment usually respond to this with pathologizing and monolithic diagnoses. However, through the heroic efforts of Bessel van der Kolk and others—like Gabor Maté in the field of addictions—this tendency has begun to change, and we can see those extremes as the product of their traumatic or neglectful histories, from which they can be released. As I'll note repeatedly, neither parts nor people are inherently flawed or destructive.

We all have these parts. And they're all valuable until they become burdened and are forced into distorted roles by what happened early in our life. IFS begins a process that allows them to totally transform back into their naturally valuable states. When that happens, not only does the part come out of its extreme role, but you now have access to its qualities and resources that you couldn't connect with before.

Parts are little inner beings who are trying their best to keep you safe.

It turns out that parts aren't afflictions and they aren't the ego. They're little inner beings who are trying their best to keep you safe and to keep each other safe and to keep it together in there. They have full-range personalities: each of them have different desires, different ages, different opinions, different talents, and different resources. Instead of just being annoyances or afflictions (which they can be while in their extreme roles) they are wonderful inner beings.

It's the natural state of the mind to have parts—they are not the product of trauma or of internalizing external voices or energies. It's just the way we're built, and that's good because all of our parts have valuable qualities and resources to give to us.

Thus, the angry part isn't a bundle of anger. If you listen to it with an open mind, you'll hear it has a lot to be angry about, but it also has fear and sadness and is just trying its best to keep you safe by being angry. Remember that parts have different desires, ages, emotions, and opinions, so they're like little inner people, and because most are quite young, they're more like inner children.

When you were young and experienced traumas or attachment injuries, you didn't have enough body or mind to protect yourself. Your Self couldn't protect your parts, so your parts lost trust in your Self as the inner leader. They may even have pushed your Self out of your body and took the hit themselves—they believed they had to take over and protect you and your other parts. But in trying to handle the emergency, they got stuck in that parentified place and carry intense burdens of responsibility and fear, like a parentified child in a family.

That's why it really helps them to realize that you're not that young age anymore. They stay stuck, however, not because they're not sure how old you are, but because they live in the past—frozen in time in the traumas that you experienced. That's why they still think they have to protect other parts who were hurt by those experiences, too, and are carrying the burdens—the extreme beliefs and emotions—from those times. They feel alone with all that pressure and terror. The simple act of turning your focus inside and beginning to listen and talk to them and let them know they aren't alone—because *you* are there to care for them—is quite radical and so welcome to that inner orphanage.

Five Things to Know About Parts

1. **Parts are innate.** Infant researchers like T. Berry Brazelton report that infants rotate through five or six states, one after the other.[1] Maybe those are the parts that are online when you're born and the others are dormant until the proper time in your development when they're needed and they kind of pop out. For example,

those of you who have kids might remember that evening when you put a compliant little two-year-old to bed and the same child woke up saying *no* to virtually everything the next morning. That assertive part debuted overnight. So it's the natural state of the mind to have parts.

2. **There aren't any bad ones.** As you get to know them, you'll learn their full range of personalities. Most are young—even the ones that dominate your life and can be quite intellectual. After parts unburden, they will manifest their true nature in valuable qualities (like delight, joy, sensitivity, empathy, wonderment, sexuality) and resources (like the ability to focus, clear discernment, problem-solving, passion for serving others or the world) that you have new access to and enrich your life.

3. **You often have to earn their trust.** The fact that they are burdened suggests that you didn't protect them in the past, and you may have locked them away or exploited them by depending on their extreme protective roles, so they usually have good reasons to not trust you. Like feral children, they need your love and nurturing, but they don't trust it at first because of their history with you. Sometimes it takes you showing up in Self repeatedly and apologizing to them to regain their trust. Fortunately, they aren't actually feral external children, so this trusting process often doesn't take more than a few visits.

4. **They can cause a lot of damage to your body and your life.** Because they're frozen in dreadful scenes in the past and carry burdens from those times, they will do whatever they need to do to get your attention when you won't listen: punish you or others, convince others to take care of them, sabotage your plans, or eliminate people in your life they see as a threat.

To do these things and more, they can exacerbate or give you physical symptoms or diseases, nightmares and strange dreams, emotional outbursts, and chronic emotional states. Indeed, most of the syndromes that make up the *Diagnostic and Statistical Manual* are simply descriptions of the different clusters of protectors that dominate people after they've been traumatized. When you think of those diagnoses that way, you feel a lot less defective and a lot more empowered to help those protectors out of those roles.

5. **They are very important and deserve to be taken seriously.** If you can establish a new, loving relationship with them and help them transform, they become wonderful companions, advisors, and playmates. You find yourself wanting to spend time with them and hear what ideas they have for you. Their conflicts don't bother you much anymore, because you know they are just parts and you can help them get along—you become a good inner parent when necessary. And it becomes a lovely life practice just to spend time with them.

Session One: Sam

I've included several transcripts of IFS sessions with clients in this book so you can get a better feel of how the work I'm describing plays out in real time. If it isn't clear, I'm the transcribed party referred to as Dick, or just D.

I teach every year at a beautiful retreat center near Big Sur, California, called Esalen. This past winter, Sam Stern (who was running their podcast at the time) asked me to do an interview with him, and he gamely agreed to let me demonstrate IFS on him. It was his first experience of IFS. If you'd like to listen to the interview, check out soundcloud.com/voices-of-esalen /dr-richard-schwartz-internal-family-systems.

DICK: So what would you like to work on?

SAM: Well, you have this piece in your work about a trailhead, taking note of an area that might be juicy or interesting to work with. I got bullied when I was in eighth grade, and the way I experienced it was that it was bad. Yeah, I took it inside myself. It felt like it shut down some pieces of me.

D: Beautiful. So do you want to focus on the pain of that? Or the shame, or do you want to focus on the part that shut you down?

S: That one—the shut down one.

D: So go ahead and find that part of you that's shut you down and see if you can find it in your body, around your body.

S: What am I looking for, Dick?

D: A numbing part maybe. . . . Here's a way to do it. As you think about going to that thirteen-year-old boy in there, what comes up in terms of fear?

S: I don't feel fear. I can see that boy and he's soft or weak and I don't feel connected to him.

D: How do you feel toward him as you see you there?

S: I don't want to be with him.

D: Okay, so focus on that feeling like you don't want to be with him and ask that part what it's afraid would happen if it let you be with him.

S: Um, it looks to me like he's scared he's gonna get physically beat. Yeah, almost like maybe afraid of me.

D: Okay, but how are you feeling toward him?

S: I want him to toughen up. He should just lash out and defend himself.

D: Right. Tell that part we understand why he'd want that, but we're going to ask him to give us the space to try and help this boy a different way and see if he'd be willing to step back and relax in there a little bit.

S: Do I actually say something to him?

D: You don't have to say it out loud, just inside, and see if you can sense that part receding or relaxing.

S: Yes, that angry lashing out part would be willing to step back.

D: As it does, how you feel toward the boy now?

S: A bit closer. Like my brother.

D: Yeah, good. Okay, so let him know that you're there to help and see how he reacts to that news.

S: Yeah! He feels good. Almost like he's more filled with life, and he's kind of peppy and cool.

D: That's great. Yeah. Okay, so ask him what he wants you to know about himself and just wait for the answer to come.

S: I'm getting that he wants to be on the baseball team. Now it's like we're friends. Yeah, he's opening up, and it's like we could have a really fun time if he slept over.

D: That's nice. Okay, Sam, then go ahead and ask him to really let you get a sense of what happened to him to make him feel bullied. Just wait for whatever he wants to give you in the way of emotion, sensations, or images.

S: He's saying that he was surprised. He was betrayed. He thought it was all cool between him and the guy, you know like they were on the same side, and then all of a sudden, he's calling to say he's going to beat the shit out of him.

D: Okay. Does that make sense to you, Sam, that that would feel terrible?

S: Sure.

D: Yeah. So let him know that you get that. And whatever else he wants to give you and what it was like for him.

S: I've done so much thinking about this that I'm having trouble separating out my assumptions around it from my memories of it.

D: Yeah. So we're going to ask the thinking part, the narrating part, to give us some space, too, just like we did the others, and see if that's possible. See if that thinking part would step out too.

S: Okay, it did.

D: Then go ahead and ask the thirteen-year-old again to really let you know what happened and how bad it was.

S: Just the rejection. I feel like I was there, and then I pulled back from it.

D: Yeah. So find the part that pulled you back.

S: He's afraid I'll feel too much. It'll be embarrassing. I'll judge myself.

D: Is he afraid of that original tough guy? He would beat you up for having cried? [*Sam agrees*] So we don't have to keep going if that's too scary, but let's ask that tough guy to go into a contained room in there for a while. Just tell him we'll talk to him afterward and let him out.

S: He gets that.

D: Okay. So now see if the part who came in to pull you away can let us go back. I promise if they really let you go all the way with this, we can heal this bullied guy so he's no longer stuck back there. He'll no longer feel bad and then they won't have to worry about him. They just need to give us the space.

S: Well, the tough guy says he'll stay in the room. Says he's ready. He's going to give us the space.

D: Okay. That's great. See if you can get back to that boy.

S: I don't feel like I'm with the boy.

D: So there's another part in the way. Just ask whoever is blocking what they're afraid would happen now if they let you be with him.

S: Not getting anything—getting more like an empty space.

D: All right. So let me talk to the part directly. Okay, so you there? Are you willing to talk to me?

S: Yes.

D: Okay, so you're the part of Sam that's blocking him from being with the boy now, is that right?

S: Yes.

D: And what are you afraid would happen if you let him go back to the boy and feel some of that?

S: Connecting to that weak boy would soften up the whole person.

D: And what would happen then if Sam was softer?

S: I'd have to change this whole person that I spent so much time constructing. I run a tight ship is what I'm trying to say. Everything works the way I do it.

D: I got it. All right, well, we don't wanna screw everything up for you. On the other hand, I think some of why you have to keep the ship so tight, of how hard you have to work, is probably because this boy is in there and you're trying to keep Sam away from him.

S: That's true.

D: And what I'm offering is the possibility of not having to work so hard because the boy is going to be feeling good.

S: Okay, but if I wasn't here, then how am I going to help Sam achieve, do everything?

D: I get that. So we won't do it without your permission, but if you're willing, I promise we can do what I just said, and you'll be freed up to do something else.

S: Yeah, well, if it'll ultimately be better for Sam, I'm into it.

D: All right, that's great. So if you don't mind going into the waiting room just till we're done and let me talk to Sam again. Sam, see if you can get close to the boy now.

S: Yes, I feel close to him.

D: Good. Let him know you're back and you're sorry that you let these parts pull you away. And tell him you're ready to know the rest of it. Everything he wants you to get about how bad it was.

S: Yeah. He feels really small. Younger than thirteen. Way younger. Yeah. Maybe like a two-year-old.

D: Okay. How do you feel toward the two-year-old?

S: Tender.

D: Nice. So let that part know, too, that you're with him and you care about him. And just see what he wants you to know.

S: I'm feeling a lot of love right now. I feel like my heart is opening. And, yeah, I'm feeling love toward the thirteen-year-old too. Like a tenderness, like a father.

D: Yeah. So let them both know.

S: It feels good. It feels really, really sweet.

D: Yeah, we can just stay with this for a while if you want. But also be open if there's something they want you to know.

S: I feel the thirteen-year-old me. I see him and he's dressed in sort of the awkward clothes of a seventh- or eighth-grade boy. Feeling that he's not pubescent or developed enough. His clothes don't look right and he couldn't defend himself right. That, like, his bones feel brittle. I don't feel disgusted by him. I'm empathizing now.

D: Let him know, and see if there's more he wants you to get about all that.

S: He wants to be funny and popular and it hurt a lot. Being bullied smacked down that idea of being popular. Really shut him down. Yeah. And I'm thinking about how later when I developed, when I was nineteen and in college, and I figured out a way to be cool, how important that was to me.

D: Of course. Just tell him you're getting all of this and see if there's more he wants you to get.

S: Yeah. There's no mean-spiritedness to him. He's not angry. He's more "just don't hurt me," but still kind of optimistic.

D: Good. But ask him if it does feel like you now get how much it did hurt. Or if there's more of that he wants you to get.

S: Yeah, I'm accessing a more "dark night of the soul" type of feeling from him and the terror.

D: Let him know you're good with that. You really want to feel it. As much as he wants you to. Does he feel like you really get how scared he was now?

S: He says he does.

D: Good. So, Sam, I want you to go into that time period and be with him in the way he needed somebody then and just tell me when you're in there with him.

S: I'm there. I'm letting him know I'm a friend—a protector.

D: Great. How is he reacting?

S: He feels good. He has somebody on his team.

D: That's right. Ask him if there's anything he wants you to do for him back there.

S: He wants me to bring him into adulthood where you can have sex and do grown-up things. He's always been interested in being in that realm.

D: Okay, we're going to do that, but first, does he want you to do anything with the bully or anything else back there before we take him out?

S: No. He doesn't seem vindictive. It doesn't seem like he wants anybody beat up.

D: All right. So let's take him wherever he wants to go. Could be the present, could be a fantasy place. Wherever he wants.

S: He wants to be at Burning Man.

D: Oh great! Okay. [*Pause*] How's he like it there?

S: A little shy.

D: Let him know that you're gonna help him learn the ropes there. And tell him he never has to go back to that bullying time again. [*Sam cries hard with relief*] Yeah. There's all the relief, right? That's great. Yeah. He never has to go back there. That's really great, Sam.

S: Amazing, man. It's like tears of joy.

D: That's really great. And he never has to go back, and you're gonna be taking care of him now.

S: It's so great. It's like what he's always wanted.

D: There you go. And ask now if he's ready to unload the feelings and beliefs he got back there that he's been carrying all this time. Ask where he carries all that in his body or around his body, throughout his body.

S: Around his head. Around his head, around his hips and heart.

D: Okay. Ask what he wants to give it all up to: light, water, fire, wind, earth, or anything else.

S: Light.

D: All right, Sam, so bring some light in and have it shine on him. And tell him to let all of that go out of his body, off his body. Just let the light take it away, no need to carry that anymore. Have him check his body, make sure he gets all of it out. Yeah. Just let it go into the light. That's right. Tell him now to invite qualities into his body that he wants and just see what comes into him now.

S: Like a pride and kindness to others. Just like a good superhero type of feel.

D: Great. So how does he seem now?

S: Like my younger friend. But safe, you know, and strong.

D: That's right. So let's let all these guys out of the waiting room and have them all come in and see him now and see how they react. Let them know they don't have to protect him or they don't have to keep you away from him anymore, so they can start thinking about new roles.

S: I see curiosity and befuddlement on the tough guy's face. He's totally confused that he's not me.

D: No, he's not you. Make that clear to him. He was beating up that kid, which wasn't good, so . . .

S: Right!

D: He needs to think about a new role now. Ask him what he'd like to do if he really trusted he didn't have to protect you like he used to.

S: Well, he's saying he's so good at everything. Can he just choose? He's really, really high on himself. Really. He sees everything that's good that I've done in my life, he's taken credit for. Yeah.

D: He can think about a new role. He doesn't have to decide right now. So how's it feeling in there now?

S: It's feeling spacious. It's feeling interesting and different.

D: Yeah. Okay. So does it feel complete for now?

S: It does, and I'm interested about how I can get in touch with this tough guy to let him know that although he is not in control of the show, he's still important to me.

D: That's exactly what you gotta tell him. You don't have to work to get in touch with him—he's around all the time. Just focus on him and talk to him about it. So. Come on back. It's a beautiful piece of work, Sam.

S: Yeah. Thank you. I was not expecting that.

I wanted to include this session because it illustrates many of the basics of IFS. For example, I repeatedly ask different protectors to open space until Sam's Self emerges and he spontaneously says he feels closer to the thirteen-year-old exile. Then he witnesses how the boy was bullied and gets the parts that try to interfere with the witnessing to step out so it can be completed. Then I have him go to the thirteen-year-old in the past and bring him to a safe place (Burning Man), and the boy is then willing to unburden the emotions he got from the bullying. The boy unburdens and transforms. And finally we bring in his most dominant protector, the tough guy, to see that the boy doesn't need his protection and he can consider a new role. Throughout, his parts increasingly came to trust in Sam's leadership.

We went from unblending parts and releasing Self to witnessing, retrieving, and unburdening an exile, and then to helping a protector consider a new role. In addition, there was a point where I talked directly to a protector, a practice we call *direct access*. While many of Sam's protectors interfered at different points, they quickly were willing to open space once he and I reassured them. This isn't true for most people—it takes longer for their protectors to trust them and me—so don't be frustrated if your sessions don't move as quickly.

I also wanted to include this session because it's a great example of how so many boys (myself included) are forced to handle their wounds and, consequently, become dominated by tough-guy parts that disdain vulnerability in themselves and others. Sam was hardly a macho guy (he does a podcast for Esalen, for God's sake!)—yet that early bullying experience and his response to it had a significant impact on his life.

As a postscript, I want to include a message Sam sent me about six months after the session:

> Personally, it was an extraordinary breakthrough for me. I've done a LOT of thinking (and feeling) about that part of me. The small boy inside of me is feeling a lot of healing and a lot of acceptance. I've done a lot of thinking about the "tough guy" and realize how deeply married I've been to him. I haven't "separated" from him,

so to speak, but am so much more conscious of his presence and my reliance on him after having apprehended, through your work, the way I've organized myself. I am curious about how he might function (as a creative? as a helper to others?) once I continue to release him from his duties as "the man!" I know, of course, that I have more work to do, and being a dad makes me want to do that.[2]

CHAPTER THREE

This Changes Everything

In Christianity, the definition of sin is anything that disconnects you from God and takes you off your path. Burdens disconnect Self from parts and give them extreme impulses. Burdened parts either don't experience Self at all or don't listen to Self. So when parts are unburdened, it's not only that they immediately transform, but they also now have much more connection to and trust for Self, which is the second goal of IFS.

When I began understanding that, I saw parallels between the inner world and the outer world. Just as people walk around feeling disconnected from each other and from whatever they call God (what I will refer to as SELF) due to the burdens (sin) they carry, parts also wander around feeling disconnected from each other and from us. Their unburdening not only allows for that reconnection inside, but it also fosters more connection between yourself and whatever you want to call the big SELF.

> It's as if there's a piece of God—for lack of a better word—in all of us and, as it turns out, in all of our parts.

As we do this kind of healing, we're not only helping ourselves not have symptoms and feel better, but we're also connecting the dots. It's as if there's a piece of God—for lack of a better word—in all of us and, as it turns out, in all of our parts.

Having done IFS with people diagnosed with Dissociative Identity Disorder, I've often found myself talking directly to one of their parts across multiple sessions. As I did that, the part would start talking about its parts, and I eventually learned that the part had a Self, as well.

At first, this was mind-blowing! Parts having parts? But after I calmed down, it made a kind of aesthetic or spiritual sense that we would have parallel or isomorphic (same form) systems at every level. It's like those Russian stacking dolls—similar systems embedded within bigger systems. Another analogy would be fractals. While it was disconcerting at first, there's something beautiful about this nested, parallel systems phenomenon for me, although I don't know how far it goes. I've actually worked with subparts of a part and came to find that it had parts too.

As I said before, I've come to see parts as sacred beings. They contain their own Self and they're worthy of the love and compassion of your Self. Back to Christianity, this seems parallel to the idea that people are created in God's image and are worthy of God's love. If people can unburden, transform into their true nature, and feel reconnected to something larger, why wouldn't it be the same for parts?

For several years we did IFS trainings for the Reformed Theological Seminary in Jackson, Mississippi, and all the students were evangelical Christians. I knew I'd be telling them that people were basically good, and so I expected them to argue that people were basically bad, and, indeed, we had that debate. I asked, "Doesn't it say in the Bible that man is created in the image of God?" They replied, "Yeah, that's true, but it's just this little seed in there and it's covered over by all this original sin." And I said, "Well, if we can translate original sin as burdens, we're talking the same language."

Their professor, Bill Richardson, summed it up nicely. "You know," he said, "I kind of know what you're trying to do here. You're asking us to do inside ourselves what Jesus did in the outside world." That is, Jesus went with compassion and curiosity and care to the exiles in the outside world and healed them—the lepers, the poor, the outcasts.

Getting back to connecting the dots, what if each of us and each of our parts contains a piece of SELF that longs to reconnect with itself? What if, by helping parts unburden and trust our Self so that we feel our connectedness to other people, to the planet, and to SELF, we are serving this larger project of divine reconnection? I think this is what IFS offers spiritual seekers. Our enlightenment is much brighter and more sustained if all of us is involved and we don't treat the ego as this bad part we have to leave behind in the dust on the way to attaining that enlightenment. Our parts long for connection to our Self—just as much as we long to connect to SELF.

Our parts long for connection to our Self—just as much as we long to connect to SELF.

When people spend time exploring inside, they all come to the same conclusion—that this essential Self is who we really are. I think that what's often called awakening or enlightenment is the embodied realization of that fact, and that shift from identifying with your parts and their burdens to identifying as your Self has profound implications.

What we're talking about transcends any particular religion and doesn't even require that you believe in something spiritual, just that you come to accept that there is this beautiful essence in you and everyone else, and that it can be accessed simply by opening space inside. Some meditations do this by emptying the mind, but in IFS, instead of wrestling with parts that don't want to be emptied, we lovingly ask them to open space inside for a few minutes and then find that Self emerges—immediately and spontaneously.

Again, this is all a lot of talk until you actually experience it for yourself, so let's shift now to some exercises that are designed to help you get to know your parts better and bring more Self to them.

Exercise: Dilemma Meditation

Once again, I invite you to get comfortable and take some deep breaths. Now, think of a dilemma in your life—either one that you're currently facing or one that you faced in the past. Pick an issue that you've experienced a lot of conflict around.

And as you focus on this dilemma, notice the parts on each side of it and notice how they battle with each other. And then notice how you feel toward that battle or toward each part in the battle. Now let's get to know each of those parts, one at a time.

To do that, you're going to ask one of them to go into a kind of waiting room. That will create a bit of a boundary that will allow the one you're currently working with to relax a little bit. So get to know the one who's not in the waiting room first. And again, notice what you're feeling toward it. If you're feeling anything negative, we're going to ask the parts associated with those negative feelings to just let you get to know it for a few minutes. We're not going to give the attended-to part more power to take over and get whatever it wants; we're just going to try to get to know it. To do that, the one you have in the waiting room (or any of its allies who are making themselves known) needs to pull its energy out of you. You can reassure it (that is, the one in the waiting room) that it'll have a time with you, too, so maybe that will help it be a little more patient.

If you *can* get to a point of at least being curious about the one who's not in the waiting room, go ahead and follow your curiosity and ask it what it wants you to know about its position. Why does it take such a strong position on this issue? What is it afraid would happen if the other one took over and won the battle? As you listen to it, you don't have to agree or disagree—just let the part know that you respect it, you care about it, you're there with it, and you hear it. See how it reacts.

In the next minute or so, I want you to ask the part you've been speaking with to go into a separate waiting room. Then let the other one out so you can get to know it in the same way. And again, you're trying to have an open heart and open mind as you listen to its side. You don't have to agree. You just kind of want to get where it's coming from, why it's so charged up about this, what it's afraid would happen if the other side won, and so on.

After you've worked with that second part for a while, ask if it would be willing to talk to the other one directly. Reassure it that you are there to mediate and to make sure they stay respectful toward each other. It's okay if the part's not willing to do that. If that happens, you won't take the next steps. But if it is willing, then invite the other one to come and sit down with the two of you.

Now you're going to kind of be their therapist as they talk to each other about this issue. And again, your job isn't to take a side—it's just to help them get to know each other in a different way and make sure they respect each other when they talk. Remind them that they're both a part of you, so they have that in common. Then, just see how they react as they get to know each other in this different way. Notice what happens to the dilemma.

At some point, pause their discussion. Let them both know that you can meet with them more regularly in this way, and ask them if they would be willing to give you their input on dilemmas in the future, but then trust you to make the final decision. They would act more like advisors for you, rather than having the responsibility of making bigger decisions like this one on their own. See how they react to that idea. As before, it can help to remind them of who you are (age-wise, etc.) and who you're not.

In the next minute or two, thank them both for however much they did and be sure to remind them that you're going to try to return. Then begin to shift your focus back to the outside world.

If your parts cooperated, it's likely you found that they really didn't know each other. This is because they've been in polarized roles with each other and had extreme visions of who the other one was. We see the same thing play out in international conflicts, as well as within countries, companies, families, and couples. The more extreme one side gets, the more the other side has to get extreme in the other direction. This process happens at all levels of human systems, particularly when there isn't good leadership, and it's no less true with inner systems. Most of us have neglected our inner worlds and we've left it to these inner children to try to make these big decisions and hash it out as we've been busy out here.

One shot at this probably isn't enough to stop the battle because the stakes feel so high for each part, and the idea of totally relaxing is anathema to them. But at least they feel a little more connected to you and to each other. This is the kind of new leadership that I'm inviting you to try out inside. Really, it's the same approach I use when working with a couple. I listen to one, then listen to the other, and in so doing, I make a connection so they both trust me. Then I bring them together, make sure they're respectful, and have them talk in this different way.

Check-In

By now I've led you through four different exercises designed to help you either get to know your parts or have them get to know you. Maybe it's gone smoothly and you're feeling pretty good about that, but it wouldn't be uncommon at all if you couldn't do one or all of the exercises, or you were only able to do pieces of them. A lot of that has to do with how ready your parts are to let you invade their world this way and how much they trust you and trust each other to open space and separate. So if they're not stepping back, for example, it doesn't mean you're failing. It simply means that it will take more time to build up their trust in you and to help them get to know you better.

If you have been able to do the exercises, it simply means that for whatever reason your parts have a certain amount of trust in you already and they're willing to open space. That's not true for all of us. Unfortunately, some of us have had plenty of terrible experiences in our lives, but that just means that it might take a little more time for our parts to trust that this type of dialogue will be useful.

At this point, you may also find yourself having strange experiences during the exercises—maybe you become unusually sleepy, find yourself thinking about other things you have to do, or get a headache. None of that is uncommon. When protectors aren't ready, they feel like they've got to distract you or take you out in some way that makes it more difficult for you to do the exercise. Don't fight them on it. My advice is to just get to know the resisting ones from this curious place—find out what they're afraid of and honor their fears.

Exercise: Working with a Challenging Protector

This exercise can prove challenging, especially if you're new to IFS work. If that's the case for you, just do your best to get to know the parts that aren't so ready.

Take a second and get comfortable, setting up like you would if you were going to meditate. Think of a part of you that really bothers you or gets in your way, one that you have a lot of shame about or one you might be afraid of. Take a second to think of one. What you're looking for is more of a protective part rather than a real vulnerable one. Some people immediately focus on their inner critics for this exercise, so if you're having trouble finding one, that usually does the job.

As you focus on the part, notice where you find it in your body or around your body, and while you focus on that place notice how you feel toward this part. Because of what you're looking for, you're probably going to have some strained feelings toward it.

Place this part of you in a contained room in there. That will help other parts of you to drop their weapons and feel a little safer. Make it a comfortable room, but one that it can't get out of and that you can see through a window. And let all these other parts that have issues with it know that for the duration of the exercise it's going to stay contained. So ask them to relax just a little bit so you can get to a point of curiosity toward the one in the room—see if they're willing to do that.

If they're not willing to separate, again, that's okay. You can spend the rest of the time just getting to know them and their fears of this other part or what issues they have with it. If you can get to a point of curiosity or any kind of openness toward the part that's in the room, then let it know that and see what it wants you to know while it stays contained. See if you can communicate with it through the window. What does it want you to know about itself? What's it afraid would happen if it stepped out of its role?

If it answered that question, then see if it's possible to extend some appreciation to it for at least trying to protect you and see how old it thinks you are. If it thinks you're a different age than you actually are, then go ahead and update it. See how it reacts.

Now, ask this part some version of the following question: "If you could change or heal what you're protecting so that it wasn't really an issue anymore and you were freed from this responsibility of protection and could do something else—what would you like to do?" That is, if the part were totally liberated from its role, what else would it choose to do? After it answers that question, ask what it needs from you in the future.

Then check with your other parts before we stop. Just see how they're reacting as they witness this conversation you had with the protector part.

When the time feels right, I invite you to finish up in there, thanking your parts for anything they let happen, letting them know this isn't your last visit. Taking deep breaths again (if that helps), shift your focus back outside.

Some years ago, I was invited to present briefly to the Dalai Lama at a conference called Mind & Life Europe. I talked with him about what I've been covering here and then I asked him a question: "Your Holiness, you ask us to offer compassion to people who are our enemies, or at least to think of them with compassion. What would it be like if we did that with our inner enemies too?" That's what this exercise is all about—to help you go to your inner enemies. Having compassion for them might be difficult at first, but ideally, we start out with an open mind and really try to get to know them.

I don't know if this happened for you, but if you stay with it and you keep asking questions that are nonthreatening, these inner enemies will reveal their secret stories of how they got forced into these roles and what they're protecting and how, in many cases, they were really heroes. As Henry Wadsworth Longfellow wrote, "If we could read the secret history of our enemies, we should find in each man's life sorrow and suffering enough to disarm all hostility."[1]

They're all good parts forced into roles they don't like.

We go to an inner enemy and listen to their secret histories and inevitably it does dissolve all the hostility in other parts of you that didn't like it. That's really great for inner enemies. They're all good parts forced into roles they don't like, they don't deserve, and they're eager to leave, but they just don't think it's safe enough to do that. Part of why they don't think it's safe is because they don't trust you as the leader. Your coming to them this way is helping to build that trust.

One more thing: You might find as you do this work that things start to shift both in your inner life and in your outer life. As you adopt this different paradigm, it's hard to look at people the same way, which means that you begin to relate to them in a different way. Some people may have trouble with these changes in you, but some people will surely welcome it.

CHAPTER FOUR

More on Systems

You may have noticed that as we proceed through the book, we're focusing less on each individual part and more on their relationships with one another. I feel blessed that when I first encountered the parts in my clients, I was steeped in what's called *systems thinking*, and that helped me listen to them better, rather than being overwhelmed with the complexity of it all. I could focus on the recurring patterns of interaction and could make sense of that. For example, I quickly saw how when a bulimic client's critic started in on her, it triggered another that felt worthless, young, alone, and empty. Then, as that one was making the client feel its feelings, to the rescue came the binge and took her away. After the binge, however, the critic returned with a vengeance, now attacking her for having binged. This, of course, triggered the young one again and my client was caught once more in that terrible cycle.

In this chapter, I'm going to cover some basic ideas of systems thinking that apply to the inner world. The information will help your inner work tremendously, and I'll be drawing on some of this material for the rest of the book.

The Growth of Systems Thinking

Systems thinking was originally developed by biologists in Europe in the 1920s who found that the method of studying cell biology by learning the laws of physics for each cell—that is, by using the traditional mechanistic, reductionistic approach—was inadequate for understanding how cells relate to each other to form living organisms. They found that the behavior of the whole system couldn't be understood from the study of each part in isolation; i.e., outside of the context of the whole system. Hence the famous saying that the "whole is greater than the sum of the parts."[1]

The systems view rapidly spread to other fields and spawned the science of ecology (which studies animal and plant communities) and cybernetics (which introduced concepts like feedback loops, self-regulation, and homeostasis). This shift from studying the makeup of objects in isolation to focusing on how the objects are embedded in networks or patterns that can be mapped does not come easily to us, because we've been raised in a more mechanistic and reductionistic paradigm. The drawing I had you create in the Mapping Your Parts exercise is one such way to map out a system.

When I first encountered systems thinking in 1976, I was thrilled to find an alternative approach to life that answered many of the questions I had about the failings I was recognizing in psychiatry. Reading Gregory Bateson and other systems theorists produced an epiphany that led me to become a family therapist and later to develop IFS. The big insight was that giving a troubled person a psychiatric diagnosis and seeing that as the sole or main cause of their symptoms was unnecessarily limiting, pathologizing, and could become self-reinforcing.

When you tell a person they are sick and ignore the larger context in which their symptoms make sense, not only do you miss leverage points that could lead to transformation, but you also produce a passive patient who feels defective. Fortunately, more people in the field are beginning to view psychiatric diagnosis as unhelpful and unscientific.[2]

Context Is Everything

Systems thinking focuses on the ways members of a system relate to one another. When you approach symptoms through that lens, you often find that they are manifestations of problems in the structure (the patterns of relationship) of the systems in which the person is embedded (family, neighborhood, work, country, etc.), as well as the system that is embedded within them (that is, their internal family). I learned as a family therapist that understanding and improving a family's structure was a far more effective and lasting way to help a child stop acting out than simply diagnosing and treating them without considering their family context.

I also found that these family structures were often maintained by extreme beliefs or emotions that were not necessarily overt but were constantly felt. For example, some of the bulimic patients' families held the belief that conflict was dangerous and the parents would become frightened whenever it arose. There was often a general disdain for neediness or vulnerability, too, and a belief that the family needed to present a perfect image to the outside world. Whatever the set of beliefs and emotions, it became a family paradigm that organized the ways the members related to each other—showing contempt when the patient was hurt, angry, or wanted attention, for example.

Larger systems are no different. The structures of corporations and countries will usually remain the same despite their dysfunctions and symptoms unless they experience a change in their basic beliefs—their paradigmatic operating systems. In the US, we'd much rather rearrange the deck chairs (taxes, environmental and immigration policy, etc.) on our national Titanic than reevaluate the underlying beliefs (for example, unlimited growth) that drive us all.

Negative (and Mistaken) Views of Human Nature

The most powerful beliefs that govern a society include the ones about human nature and the way the world works. These are often unstated and unchallenged because they are assumed to be reality—just the way things are. As Donella Meadows states, "Growth is good. Nature is a stock of resources to be converted to human purposes. Evolution stopped with the emergence of *Homo sapiens*. One can 'own' land. These are a few of the paradigmatic assumptions of our current culture, all of which have utterly dumbfounded other cultures, who thought them not the least bit obvious."[3]

Most of a society's rules and goals trickle down from its assumptions about whether people are basically good or evil, competitive or collaborative, trustworthy or selfish, isolated or interconnected, hopeless or redeemable, inferior or superior. All of these views affect a given society's members.

You're probably familiar with the placebo effect, but the opposite (called the *nocebo effect*) is equally real and powerful. For example, if you believe a sugar pill will make you sick, you'll probably get sick. Applied to human relations, there is ample evidence that our negative expectations of others have a strong negative impact on their behavior or performance.[4] This can easily initiate vicious reinforcing feedback loops in which negative expectations become self-fulfilling prophesies that further reinforce the negative views, and so on. This is one reason why racism is so pernicious.

As discussed in the introduction, the view of humanity that has dominated the Western world trends toward the pessimistic. In order to justify slavery, white Europeans started to differentiate themselves from other less "civilized" cultures; we might all struggle with primitive impulses, but according to that paradigm, some (typically darker) people were not as skilled at controlling their irrational, bestial parts. This veneer theory of controlling the primitive can be applied not only to impulses but also to people. One theme of this book is that how we think about and relate to the inhabitants of our inner worlds translates directly to how we think about and relate to people. If we live in fear of and strive to control certain parts of us, we will do the same to people who resemble those parts.

The veneer theory suggests that civilization forms the protective layer necessary to contain and hide all our primitive instincts that are constantly wanting to break through. Historian Rutger Bregman asserts that, in contrast to the veneer theory, people are basically good. He debunks the research of notable thinkers such as Richard Dawkins, Philip Zimbardo, and Stanley Milgram—all of whom held extremely pessimistic (and highly influential) views about people. When Bregman took a second look at the methods and data from their famous studies, he found enough rampant distortion and falsification to discredit them outright.

Bregman's argument is that we have organized all our institutions based on this selfish view of people and that if we realized that wasn't true, everything would change. Once we shift paradigms to the knowledge that, at their essence, everyone is decent and kind, we can reorganize our economic systems, schools, and prisons. He offers many examples of successful institutions and programs that are based on the positive view of human nature—the prison system in Norway, for example, that has the lowest recidivism rate in the world. In contrast to American prisons, guards in Norway are taught to make friends with the inmates and help prepare them for normal life. Meanwhile, the number of people incarcerated in the US has grown over 500 percent since 1972, to the point where the US jails almost a quarter of the world's prisoners. Speaking of racism, nearly 60 percent of these prisoners are black or Latinx.[5]

Clearly, our veneer-based approach of control and contain isn't working. What if it was true that there are no bad parts, only burdened ones frozen in the past that needed to be unburdened rather than punished? What if, at their essence, everyone was a Self that could be accessed quickly? How would the world be different?

Why the Negative View Doesn't Work

Going to war against (coercing, harshly punishing, or shaming, for example) any social problem sets in motion reinforcing feedback loops that have the potential to destroy the system, because they escalate over time and drain the system's resources.

This is true in the inner world, as well. Going to war against protector parts only makes them stronger. Listening to them and loving them, however, helps them heal and transform. The challenge here is that we are dominated—individually and collectively—by hardline, punitive parts who believe that people (and their parts) are basically bad and need to be warred against. If you believe that within you are dangerous, bestial, or sinful impulses that need to be constantly monitored, controlled, and, if necessary, battled against (the veneer theory adopted for the inside world), then it makes sense that you would see other people that way, and your approach to social problems will invariably involve controlling tactics and war.

Time and again, we've seen how leaders of one country demonize the people in another land to justify going to war against them. As Charles Eisenstein puts it, "There are so many fights, crusades, campaigns, so many calls to overcome the enemy by force. . . . Thus it is that the inner devastation of the Western psyche matches exactly the outer devastation it has wreaked upon the planet."[6]

I developed IFS while working with clients suffering from eating disorders, where the most common approach to treating these people remains focused on "defeating" their disorder (with expected results). Our cultural war on drugs, as well, has been an unmitigated disaster with massive unintended consequences throughout the world. We need a new approach based on no longer trying to kill the messenger and instead listening to the message—no longer going to war against nature or human nature.

This view—that people have a sinful, aggressive, selfish, impulsive nature that must be controlled by their rational minds (or by help from God)—also leads to a profound sense of disconnection from other people and disdain for oneself. If everyone is out for themselves, then you should be too. You have to protect yourself. You shouldn't be too open and naïve. You need to watch your back. The problem here is that this approach doesn't work. It only leaves you feeling lonely, ashamed, and afraid—feelings you think you have to hide for fear of being rejected. When you believe you are a separate, selfish, and sinful soul among other wretches like yourself, it's hard to not feel lonely, even when with people. When you're alone with your pathetic self, you feel even more rejected and worthless and, consequently, are likely to withdraw even more.

What if, instead, you knew that your loneliness was held by another part of you? What if you identified with your Self rather than your exiles? And what if you saw the Self in everyone around you?

Feedback Loops

I spoke about legacy burdens in chapter one. There are four in particular—racism, patriarchy, individualism, and materialism—that have dominated our country's mindset since the founders brought them from Europe. Each of these legacy burdens combines with the others to create the pervasive sense that we are all disconnected and on our own in a dangerous, dog-eat-dog world. In turn, they create what systems theorists call a *reinforcing feedback loop*. The sense of competitive separateness (and the belief that anyone with enough willpower can make it) leads people to exile and disdain those who do less well than them. In turn, this creates even more separateness and fear for survival in the system, which leads to more exiling, and so on.

One reinforcing feedback loop that is common in all kinds of systems is called *success for the successful*. As applied to our country's division of wealth, we find that those with more privilege, accumulated capital, inside information, and special access and influence are able to create more privilege, capital, access, and information. On the other hand, those without those advantages become exiled, and as such, they and their children get worse educations, have trouble getting loans with reasonable interest rates, are subject to red-lining practices, and are discriminated against because of race or class. Furthermore, their voices are rarely heard by politicians, who are typically more concerned with the influential members of society, i.e., the wealthy. Unfortunately, as Meadows warns, "A system with an unchecked reinforcing feedback loop ultimately will destroy itself."[7]

However, there is another important kind of feedback loop in all living systems that is necessary for their survival. Organisms need to maintain homeostasis (steady state) in various vital processes. For humans, these include body temperature, blood sugar, oxygen levels, blood pressure, et cetera. When any of those variables go outside of a healthy range, receptors are triggered, setting in motion a feedback process which brings the variable back within it. In contrast to reinforcing feedback loops, which result in escalations of a variable, those that restore homeostasis are called *stabilizing* or *balancing feedback loops*. For example, if your blood sugar level gets too high, your pancreas is notified to produce more insulin until your sugar level returns to the healthy range.

If we think of the Earth as a living system or being—as Gaia—then the COVID-19 pandemic could be seen as part of a stabilizing feedback loop. For 99 percent of human history, the human species has not been a dire threat to the health of the planet. Starting with the Industrial Revolution, the world's human population—and its ability to exploit the planet's resources—has exploded in the last two centuries. Since the late 1880s, we've been riding on different runaway reinforcing feedback loops, and because they've improved the lives of most people in tangible ways, we've become convinced of the myth of the march of progress. Unfortunately, the march hasn't been so progressive for the rest of the planet.

We've lost our ability to feel the Earth viscerally. Through our extractive, exiling, and disconnecting attitudes and behaviors, we've lost our ability to feel the Earth viscerally. Our receptors are numbed to the feedback the Earth has been offering us for decades, telling us time and again that she isn't happy or healthy. It's not that she hasn't informed us—there have been plenty of signs. It's that the striving, coercive parts that came to dominate much of our species have been too focused on financial and material gain to heed those signs. We stopped caring about the Earth and instead viewed her as a set of resources to be used however we wanted. But there are consequences to this.

That brings us back to the pandemic. As a group of biodiversity experts notes: "Rampant deforestation, uncontrolled expansion of agriculture, intensive farming, mining and infrastructure development, as well as the exploitation of wild species have created a 'perfect storm' for the spillover of diseases from wildlife to people." They warn that 1.7 million unidentified viruses known to infect people are estimated to exist in mammals and water birds. Any one of these may be more disruptive and lethal than COVID-19. They suggest that a beginning step is for countries to recognize complex interconnections among the health of people, animals, plants, and our shared environment. Additionally, we need to prop up healthcare systems in the most vulnerable countries where resources are strained and underfunded.[8] In other words, they are asking leaders of countries to become systems thinkers.

Maybe climate crises and viruses are built-in stabilizing feedback mechanisms that kick in whenever our species exceeds the planet's homeostatic range. This speculation may come across as cold-blooded, and I certainly don't want to diminish the unbelievable amount of suffering and death the pandemic has caused throughout the world to date. My primary intention here is to make a plea for us to quickly learn the lessons of this crisis so we can end it as quickly as possible and avoid worse disasters in the future.

If our species can finally get the message and shift our values and priorities, maybe we can avoid worse stabilizing feedback from Mother Earth. Maybe we can start listening to and respecting her again. But we can't do that without a dramatic paradigm shift. Our fate isn't in our own hands; it's in our minds.

Everything Is Connected

As Eisenstein urges, we must discard the "Story of Separation" and adopt the "Story of Interbeing."[9] We need systems-thinking leaders who can remind everyone that we're all in this together.

I often ask clients to have their polarized parts come together to talk directly to one another. The first question I have the client ask each part is whether they have anything in common. Each part is often shocked to learn that they share the desire to keep the person safe, but their ideas about how to do that are totally different. With the realization that they are interconnected, they become committed to working together better for the well-being of the larger system (the client) they both inhabit. Likewise, helping people—in families, companies, countries, and internationally—realize their connectedness brings forth the Self at each of those levels, and the Self always brings healing. Meadows reminds us of how we are all interconnected. "No part of the human race is separate either from other human beings or from the global ecosystem."[10]

We need systems-thinking leaders who can remind everyone that we're all in this together.

If the planet's climate collapses, everyone will suffer—even the rich. If the workers in a company are overstressed, the company will fail and the owners will go bankrupt. If you are dominated by your brain and neglect the rest of your body, you will get sick and your brain will go down with the ship. Having a huge poor population either drains most of a country's resources or creates violent social upheaval. If you exile your vulnerable parts, they will destroy you.

The Shift

Currently, we view ourselves and our fellow humans as fundamentally selfish and flawed, which leads to dog-eat-dog, ruthless economic and social systems. And because we approach our problems out of context (that is, non-systemically), our attempted solutions to those problems often make things worse—namely, harming the planet and creating masses of exiled people. Exiling is toxic to any system. It severs our connection to each other, to our own bodies, to the Earth, and to the divine.

Our inner world is also polluted by this paradigm. Our treasury of parts ends up mirroring the external system—with lots of exiles, lots of protectors who disdain them, and with our burdens as the fundamental organizing principle of our inner system, as opposed to our Self. Clearly, this way of being with ourselves and the world is not sustainable. Here's the alternative paradigm that I'm proposing:

Within each of us is a wise, compassionate essence of goodness that knows how to relate harmoniously. In addition, we're not one messed-up mind, but an internal system of parts. Sure, these parts can sometimes be disruptive or harmful, but once they're unburdened, they return to their essential goodness. And because this is true, each of us has a clear path in front of us to access and lead our lives—inner and outer—from that essence. In doing so, we realize the basic truth of interconnectedness on all levels, and the natural result of that realization is compassion and courageous action.

I know it sounds like a lot. But making this paradigm shift doesn't actually require huge sacrifices or suffering. It can be painful to retrieve parts of yourself that you left in the dust, but the effort is more than worth it. Here's just a taste of what you have to gain: more love for yourself and others, more access to your inner joy and delight (as well as to your rich sadness and grief), and more meaningful habits and activities with a sense of fulfilling vision.

Exercise: Daily IFS Meditation

Here's a meditation that I and other IFS practitioners use to foster this paradigm shift within us. I encourage you to practice some version of it on your own every day.

Start by taking a second to get comfortable. If it helps you to go inside to take some deep breaths, go ahead and do that. If you've tried out the exercises earlier in the book, hopefully by now you're getting to know a handful of your parts. I'm going to invite you to focus on the ones that you're getting to know first. And the goal of focusing on them is really just to follow up and see how they're doing now and if there's anything they need, if there's more they want you to know. This is all in service of building an ongoing relationship with your parts so they feel more connected to you, less isolated and alone.

At some point, remind them that you're there with them, that you care about them, and tell them a little more about who you are, because even as you work with parts, they often forget these things until they've been unburdened. And it never hurts to just remind them that they're not alone anymore and that you're not a young child anymore and that you can care for them in a way they need.

The goal is to take your parts as seriously as you take your literal children, if you have children. The good news is that your parts don't need nearly as much maintenance or nurturance as literal children do—they often just need to know about this connection you're building, just to be reminded of it.

Then at some point you can expand your purview and invite any other parts that need attention to come to you. On different days, different parts will show up. Just get to know them and what they need from you, and also let them know who you are and that they're not alone anymore.

And then this next piece is optional in each meditation: If you'd like to, you can revisit each of these parts, inviting them to relax inside in open space just for a few minutes, and ask them to trust that it's safe to let you more into your body. Their energy tends to make it harder for you to be embodied when they're triggered. And if they're willing to let you in more, you'll notice a shift each time they relax—you'll feel more space inside your mind and body. Remind them that it's just for a few minutes, that it's just an experiment to see what happens if they let you be there more. They don't have to if they don't want to, in which case you can just continue to get to know them. But if they are willing, notice the qualities of this increase in spaciousness and embodiment. Notice what it feels like to be more in your body with a lot of space.

You might notice a shift in your breathing or your ability to be present. You might feel your muscles relax and a sense of well-being, like everything's okay. And as I said before, you might also notice a kind of energy running through your body, making your extremities tremble a little bit or tingle. I'm very auditory, so I can also notice a shift in my tone of voice while I'm in this state. I also enjoy the peace that comes with the lack of a pressing agenda.

If your parts are having a lot of trouble relaxing, it just means that they need more of that kind of attention at some point. So let them know you get it, that there's no pressure for them to do anything. When the time feels right, you can begin to shift your focus back out here, thank your parts for whatever they let you know, and remind them you're going to do this practice more in the future. Take some deep breaths if that helps you come out.

As I go through my day, I often pause and notice how much I'm in this state. When I'm not, it means there's some part that's taken over or is at least more active, and I can quickly find that part and remind it that it's safe to trust me, that it can relax a little bit and open more space. It's taken a while, but almost in every situation now my parts do that pretty readily and I can feel the energy again and the spaciousness, and I can relate to people from that place.

This becomes a daily practice. In addition to noticing the parts and helping them trust that it's safe to open space, it's usually necessary to actively work with them and do some healing, because as long as your system is vulnerable, it'll be hard for them to trust you. So in combination with this meditation, I and other IFS practitioners will actively do sessions to unburden parts.

CHAPTER FIVE

Mapping Our Inner Systems

N ow that you have several practices under your belt and understand more about systems and the paradigm shift we're after here, I want to get into some of the ways parts organize themselves and relate with each other inside. I've already introduced the primary distinction between exiles and protectors. Let's look a little more into what those parts are like.

Exiles

Let's start with the exiles. These are often the younger ones that have frequently been called inner children in our culture. Before we get hurt, they are the delightful, playful, creative, trusting, innocent, and open parts of us that we love to be close to. They are also the most sensitive parts, so when someone hurts, betrays, shames, or scares us, they are the parts who take in the extreme beliefs and emotions (burdens) from those events the most.

After the trauma or attachment injury, the burdens these parts absorb shift them from their fun, playful states to chronically wounded inner children who are frozen in the past and have the ability to overwhelm us and pull us back into those dreadful scenes. They move from feeling "I am loved" to "I am worthless" and "No one loves me," and when they blend with us, that belief becomes our paradigm and we feel all their burdened emotions. It feels unbearable to reexperience those emotions and to believe those things, and, often, those burdens impair our ability to function in the world. I've had clients who, when their exiles took over, couldn't get out of bed for a week.

Those burdens impair our ability to function in the world.

This is why we try our best to lock these parts away, thinking that we are simply moving on from bad memories, sensations, and emotions—not realizing that we are disconnecting from our most precious resources just because they got hurt. This is because we are imbued with the mono-mind paradigm that doesn't allow for the idea of hurt parts that can be healed, not to mention our American rugged individualism that says when you get hurt, the best course of action is to pick yourself up and move on.

Indeed, it's likely that after you were hurt, the people around you gave you some version of that message: "Just get over it," for example, or "Stop being so sensitive." For these young parts, that's just adding insult to injury. The injury came from the event and then you insult them by abandoning and imprisoning them. As a result, they are often quite desperate to be attended to and will try their best to break out of exile any chance they get—when we're tired, when we're not getting the accolades that keep them pacified, or when we're hurt or shamed in a way that's similar to the original event.

This is such an unnecessary tragedy. These delightful inner children are hurt and then abandoned, and we no longer have access to their wonderful qualities. Instead, we assume that it's part of becoming an adult to no longer feel intense joy, awe, and love.

Even when they are exiled, their burdens can exert an unconscious effect on our self-esteem, choice of intimate partner, career, and so on. They're behind the overreactions that seem mysterious to us and leave us perplexed as to why certain small things hit us so hard.

It's very hard to grow up in the US without accumulating a number of exiles. As a child, you were almost certainly hurt, humiliated, or terrified multiple times by your family or peers and were then coldly expected to just move on. Abuse survivors inevitably have many exiles.

In addition to the vulnerable parts of us that get hurt and then exiled, there are other lively and protective parts that don't fit in our families, or maybe they scare people around us. Those become what I call *protectors-in-exile*. Robert Bly writes eloquently about these parts:

> A child running is a living globe of energy. We had a ball of energy, all right; but one day we noticed that our parents didn't like certain parts of that ball. They said things like: "Can't you be still?" or "It isn't nice to try to kill your brother." Behind us we have an invisible bag, and the part of us our parents don't like, we, to keep our parents' love, put in the bag. By the time we go to school our bag is quite large. Then our teachers have their say: "Good children don't get angry over such little things." So we take our anger and put it in the bag. By the time my brother and I were twelve in Madison, Minnesota, we were known as "the nice Bly boys." Our bags were already a mile long. . . . When we put a part of ourselves in the bag it regresses. It de-evolves toward barbarism. Suppose a young man seals a bag at twenty and then waits fifteen or twenty years before he opens it again. What will he find? Sadly, the sexuality, the wildness, the impulsiveness, the anger, the freedom he put in have all regressed; they are not only primitive in mood, they are hostile to the person who opens the bag. The man who opens his bag at forty-five or the woman who opens her bag rightly feels fear. She glances up and sees the shadow of an ape passing along the alley wall; anyone seeing that would be frightened. Every part of our personality that we do not love will become hostile to us.[1]

These exiles are what Freud famously called the *Id*, and he mistakenly assumed they were merely primitive impulses. As I discussed earlier, that negative take just added to Western culture's detrimental view of human nature and was highly influential in psychotherapy's disinterest in getting to know those parts of us.

Once you have a lot of exiles, you feel far more delicate and the world seems more dangerous because there are so many things and people and situations that could trigger them. And when an exile gets triggered and bursts out of whatever container we keep it in, it can feel like we're about to die, because it was exactly that scary or humiliating when the originating event happened. Or maybe, as Bly notes, we're terrified because the exiles have become so extreme.

I'll write more on this topic later, but for now I just want to note that in terms of spiritual preferences, our exiles' sense of worthlessness is likely to unconsciously steer us toward spiritualities or gurus that promise redemption or salvation. Similarly, because of their fear and hurt, we might tend toward forms of worship that are centered around a guru or some notion of an all-powerful God.

Managers

When you have a lot of exiles, other parts of you will have to leave their valuable roles to become protectors. It's like your adolescent parts are pressed into military or police service. Some of them take on the role of controlling the outside world so that nothing triggering happens—they manage our relationships, appearance, and performance often by yelling at us the way our parents or teachers once did so that **Managers are parentified inner children.** we'll try harder or look better. These are the parts that become inner critics. Other parts take another approach and try to take care of everyone else while neglecting ourselves. Others are hypervigilant, and some are intellectual and are skilled at keeping us out of our bodies. There are many common roles these manager parts take. What they all have in common is the desire to preempt the triggering of our exiles by controlling, pleasing, or disconnecting us.

So managers are one class of protectors. These parts carry heavy burdens of responsibility for which they are ill-equipped because they are young too. In family therapy, we call children who take on these adult duties parentified children.

Managers are parentified inner children. They are usually very tired and stressed out. They're trying to keep the world safe for our exiles while at the same time keeping our exiles contained. They also have the ability to numb our bodies so we don't feel so much, because if you don't feel, then you don't get triggered. Managers are working all the time—some of them never sleep.

Other managers don't want us to feel good about ourselves for fear that we'll take risks and get hurt. They protect us by tearing us apart. They are the self-hating parts of us who will sabotage anything that might make us feel good. They may let us try meditation or other spiritual practices, but usually just to reduce stress rather than to commune with the nondual. If the practice helps them contain the exiles (as in a managerial spiritual bypass), they're all for it. Mainly, they want to keep us small, because the safest place to be is below the radar.

In general, managers don't like anything that takes us out of their control and, as I mention above, some don't like anything that makes us open our hearts and feel confident or good about ourselves. On the other hand, there are managers who want to belong and to please everyone. These are the parts that make us go regularly to church, for example, but they're not all that interested in directly experiencing the divine.

Firefighters

Firefighters are another class of protectors entirely. Despite how hard our managers work to prevent it, the world has a way of triggering our exiles at times, of breaking through what psychotherapy traditionally calls our defenses. When that happens, it's a big emergency. To many of your protectors, experiencing the pain of your exiles feels like you might die. Consequently, most of us have a set of parts whose job it is to deal with these emergencies, parts who will immediately go into action to put out that inner fire—the flames of emotion bursting out from the exiled place.

In contrast to the managers who try to preempt anything that's going to trigger the exiles, these firefighter parts are activated after an exile has been triggered and desperately (and often impulsively) try to douse the flames of emotion, get us higher than the flames with some substance, or find a way to distract us until the fire burns itself out.

Depending on how much you fear your exiles, your firefighters will resort to desperate measures with little regard for the collateral damage to your health or your relationships. All they know is they have to get you away from those feelings right now or else! Sometimes their fears of your death are warranted, because suicide is an option for some firefighters if other solutions don't work.

I referred to spiritual bypassing in chapter one. Many people come to meditation to escape their feelings, and I find the use of spiritual practices to transcend one's exiles to be rampant in the communities I treat. Your firefighters will get you addicted to the practice in part because it's a great solution for them. You feel good as long as you do it and, unlike other addictions on the menu, no one is upset with you for doing it, including your own managers. In fact, people admire or envy your discipline and see you as holy. Unlike managers, firefighters love going into the higher realms and losing control—the further from your pain the better. In those higher realms you can access a lot of pure Self, which feels great—even though it doesn't heal anything and can make exiles feel even more abandoned.

I find the use of spiritual practices to transcend one's exiles to be rampant in the communities I treat.

Where exiles are often desperate for redemption, firefighters are like babysitters for those younger parts— babysitters who can't get the kids to stop screaming or giving your system waves of anxiety or shame. For this reason, firefighters are desperate to find someone to make the exiles feel better, and often become recruiters who search for that special person or practice. They turn us into seekers who move from one meditation or spiritual leader to another, looking for the one that can permanently make those exiles feel better. Or, if they find one that seems to do the trick, they become zealous advocates and followers. Many people come to spiritual traditions with lots of exiles because of the intense trauma in their backgrounds, hoping for relief. Unfortunately, many spiritualities don't know what to do with people's traumas other than to help them bypass them.

One last thing about firefighters. For us to live in this culture and not see the suffering of its exiles or feel the outrage of what we are doing to the Earth, we need distractions. We are provided with a plethora of firefighter activities to help us numb the pain of this moral injury. Remember, Self sees, feels, and acts to change injustice, so to not do any of that we need illegal drugs or prescription medications, constantly available media entertainment, all-consuming jobs, and spiritual bypasses.

I'm not trying to hold myself up as a model of Self-leadership in this regard. I spend more time watching Netflix and the Boston Celtics than protesting in the streets. I comfort myself that promulgating IFS is doing something important, but I still need my firefighters to keep me from fully absorbing what's happening in the world and devoting all my time and energy to activism.

I want to reiterate here that these categories—exiles, managers, and firefighters—do not describe the essence of your parts. They're simply the roles these parts were forced into by what happened to you.

Returning to the systems ideas of reinforcing and stabilizing feedback and homeostasis, managers are commonly your system's homeostatic mechanisms. Whenever your behavior or inner experience strays from what they believe is safe for you, they act to bring you back. For example, if many of your parts carry the burden that the world is very dangerous and it's best to stay invisible, when you start to feel good about yourself, your critic will tear you down out of fear that you'll start taking risks. If the critic gets overridden, then other managers kick in—maybe you dissociate or fall asleep. Many would-be meditators who feel like failures because they struggle with the practice turn out to be carrying that burden. Parts won't let them meditate because they don't think opening the heart is a good idea.

We all have burdens that are committed to keeping us safe and homeostatic.

In this example, the variable your managers are containing within a homeostatic range is your self-worth. In other people it might be anger, sadness, exuberance, or neediness. In still others, it's behaviors like spontaneous movement or speech, assertiveness, or vulnerability. We all have burdens that are committed to keeping us safe and homeostatic. They differ in the kind of stabilizing feedback activities they use but not in their intentions.

In some ways, firefighters generally seem to be part of reinforcing feedback loops, because their activities often take you far out of your managers' comfortable, homeostatic range. Then those managers will do their best to bring you back. Indeed, the reinforcing loop is often between firefighters and managers—the harder managers try to control them, the stronger firefighters become, which can escalate to your death in some cases. Yet firefighter behavior itself is usually homeostatic in the sense that its original purpose was to squelch or distract from the exiled feelings until they are back within a tolerable range.

The triggering of exiles often kicks off reinforcing feedback cycles, because attempts to stifle them from either managers or firefighters will make them try harder to break out or get your attention. What begins as a slight headache becomes a raging migraine, for example, when your managers convince you to ignore the exile's first attempt to get your attention.

The point here is that thinking systemically and tracking inner sequences of parts' activities that surround problems allows you to avoid the mistake of, for example, colluding with your managers to further repress your firefighters or exiles—taking an aspirin instead of listening inside to your exiles' pain. Or you and your therapist won't overreact if, after you do listen and feel the exiled pain, the next day you feel suicidal or want to go get drunk. Instead, you and your therapist trust that the exile work must have triggered a firefighter you didn't get permission from who is now afraid and is simply acting in a homeostatic way. Again, traumatized inner systems are delicate ecologies. Just like with external ecologies, changes in one aspect can have unforeseen consequences. This is far less likely, however, if you think in terms of systems—then the consequences often can be foreseen and preempted or dealt with from Self.

Of course, this map doesn't just apply to inner systems. It has been used effectively to understand and work with families and corporations, and I believe it applies to human systems at any level. Systems of parts and people tend to polarize, form protective alliances, and exclude or cut off from each other whenever they are traumatized and lack effective leadership.

The exercises in this book are mainly focused on helping you get to know and appreciate your protectors. It can be quite a bit trickier to open up to your exiles by yourself. If you do begin to feel overwhelmed with exiled feeling, it's important to shift out of the exercise. In most cases it works to get to know who some of your exiles are, but we're not inviting you to actually get close to them and try to help them, because most people, including myself, need to have somebody with them to do that—ideally an IFS therapist (see the directory on ifs-institute.com), or at least someone who can stay in Self while you get emotional.

I learned many years ago the importance of respecting protectors and their right to protect the system and to not be pushed out of the way. Burdened inner systems are sensitive environments and we need to approach and visit them accordingly. Your protectors have spent a lifetime trying to keep you (and everyone else) away from your exiles, so they need to be consulted first and convinced that there is a good reason to let you go there. We don't go to exiles without permission from protectors.

I learned this the hard way in the early days of developing IFS. As clients described having parts that were in intense pain or terror, it seemed like those were the ones that needed to heal, so I steered my clients toward them as soon as I could and when we succeeded in getting there, we were unknowingly bypassing their protectors. As we'll see with Mona soon, some clients experienced severe backlash reactions (suicidal impulses, physical pain or fevers, episodes of self-hate, or distrust of me) as the protectors punished them for our transgression. This is why we've learned to be ecologically sensitive guests in our clients' ecosystems.

We don't go to exiles without permission from protectors.

That's partly why I'm laying this map out now, so that as you continue with the exercises, you can keep in mind where we are and where we're headed. Again, it's a fairly simple map: exiles, managers, firefighters. The only other category you might find in yourself are the protectors-in-exile I briefly mentioned. These are parts that are not young and vulnerable. Instead, they are often impulsive firefighters that your managers locked up because they hurt someone or have that potential. Or because you were raised with parents or in a culture that shamed you for having those parts. Often you will be very frightened of and have distorted views of these parts until you begin to listen to them and find that they are no different from other protectors. They need your help too.

Once again, I want to remind you that the categories I describe in this map don't capture the essence of your parts themselves. Instead, they are just the roles your parts were thrust into because of what happened in your childhood. They are maintained by the burdens they carry and by where they are frozen in the past. When retrieved, unburdened, and released from these roles, these parts become something quite different and always valuable. It's often hard to predict what they'll transform into. A manager might just want to lie on the beach, and a firefighter might want to use its energy for something healthy and playful rather than on getting you drunk.

Session Two: Mona

I was recently asked to offer a consult session for an IFS therapist whose client, Mona, had a psychotic break four years earlier and was interested in exploring the parts that might have been involved with that, but she was also quite afraid to. Mona told me that during that prior episode she'd been hospitalized and put on antipsychotics and diagnosed as having bipolar disorder. She had rebuilt her life since then, but she was still medicating for fear of a relapse and wanted to see if IFS could help her understand what happened and gain confidence that it wouldn't come back.

With her therapist (Bob) with her on the Zoom call, I ask Mona to focus on the manic part and find it in her body. She locates it in her chest and sees an image of herself in the psych ward, feeling trapped and desperate. I ask how she feels toward that younger woman and she says she feels sorry for her and wants to hold her there. I tell her to do that and she does, but suddenly she shifts away from the scene and says she's sleepy. I ask to talk directly to the part that's taking her away with sleep and ask it why it is afraid to let her stay with that part in the hospital. It says it's afraid that manic part will take over again and she'll wind up back where she was. I tell it that makes sense, but that I know how to keep it from taking over and instead we'll help it not have to be in this manic role. The sleepy dissociative part recedes, and Mona returns to holding the woman in the hospital.

Suddenly, she sees a giant abyss and is afraid of it. I ask her to get the scared parts into a waiting room and assure her that her therapist and I will be with her if she wants to go into that black hole. She now feels curious and wants to enter with us. We enter and she sees a hand reaching out from the dark. She takes the hand and we leave the hole and find that the hand is attached to a four-year-old girl. Mona embraces the girl and spontaneously apologizes to her for throwing her in the hole. I tell her to ask the girl what happened to her in the past. A protector jumps in to say that it was the girl's fault.

I talk directly to the protector and ask where it got that idea. It says that her parents always stressed how she and her sisters were responsible for what they allowed boys to do to them. I tell the part that it's understandable that it would believe what the parents said and would want to protect them, but that we need to help the four-year-old unload all her feelings and we won't auto-matically believe what she shows about what happened—we'll just heal her.

Mona suddenly sees the girl, naked and outside, and she isn't sure how she got there. I tell her to ask the girl. "There was a teenager who came to live with my family. She says he did something to her, but she doesn't know what because she left—she dissociated—went to sleep." I say, "Yeah, that same sleepy dissociating part protected her then the way it's been trying to do today. We need to remember to thank it for saving you." I tell Mona to enter the scene and be with the girl in the way she needed at the time. She does and gets the girl in some clothes and brings her out of the scene to the present and helps her unburden the shame and terror she'd been carrying since that time.

The girl feels very happy now and wants to play. I tell Mona to bring in the manic woman in the hospital to see that the girl is doing well, and the woman takes off her hospital gown and unburdens the manic feelings. Mona says, "I think when I was experiencing psychosis, parts of my brain were grasping some of this, but it was too much." We end the session with the homework that Mona is to make a daily practice of checking on these parts every day for at least a month. She says she feels lighter and relieved.

However, several hours later I get a panicky call from her therapist saying that Mona is suicidal. He asks me to talk to her again.

DICK: What's happening?

MONA: I was driving home and felt intensely suicidal. There's a part that's furious with me and wants to kill me.

D: All right, let's work with it. Let me talk to it so we can see what it wants us to know. Are you there?

M: Mona's a stupid fucking bitch! I hate her so much! I hate her so much! I just want her to die! I want to hurt her and hit her!

D: [*Calmly*] Why? Tell me why?

M: She does everything wrong!

D: What are you afraid would happen if you didn't kill her or hurt her?

M: She'd just keep fucking everything up.

D: What did she fuck up?

M: [*Crying*] She can't get us the kind of love that we need because she messes up everything. Every relationship.

D: All right, but tell me why you're so upset with her now. Is it related to the work we did?

M: She's making everyone see that she's exposed and naked.

D: So what was that like for you to have her expose that?

M: It's the worst thing that could ever happen! She needs to be strong and perfect.

D: How old do you think she is?

M: [*As Mona*] She says I'm thirty-two. I'm telling her I'm a lot older than that now.

D: Great. I suspect that when you were thirty-two, she had good reasons to keep you strong and perfect. Is that right? And to attack you if you ever did let your guard down.

M: Yeah, I got depressed then and I totally shut down and lost everything and it went on for years.

D: Is she relieved to learn that you're not in that place now?

M: No, because she says I'll probably just keep fucking up and getting hurt.

D: Okay. Let me talk directly to the part again. [*To the part:*] How has it been to talk to me about these feelings you have?

M: It's good to tell someone how stupid she is.

D: No—what you've told me is how dangerous it is for her to expose herself and be vulnerable, and we get that. And we get that there were times when you really needed to keep her from doing that. How's it feel to hear that?

M: It feels good.

D: Thank you for sharing all that with me and let me talk to Mona again. Are you there? [*She nods*] How do you feel toward this part now?

M: I feel affection for it—it's just trying to keep me in line.

D: Yeah, it's just trying to keep you safe—it doesn't really want to kill you. It doesn't know what else to do but threaten you to get you to behave. Let it know you get that and see how it reacts now.

M: It's feeling relief.

D: And do update it about your life now and how there are people you can trust to be vulnerable with, like Bob [her therapist].

M: Yeah, she's crying and exhausted. I'm asking her where she got these beliefs about having to be perfect and strong. She says it was in my twenties. I'm holding her while she cries. She feels embarrassed for her outburst.

D: No need to. It's great you found her too. And I'm glad you guys called me, and I'll hand it back to Bob now.

B: Thanks, Dick. Mona, how do you feel toward that part now?

M: Very maternal—I'm still holding her.

The reason I included this session is probably clear: no matter how much we check with protectors upfront and seem to get permission from them, it's not uncommon for firefighters like Mona's to backlash afterward. If something like this happens with you, instead of polarizing the part and initiating a reinforcing feedback loop, try getting curious instead. In my experience, the part just needs to be understood, reassured, and loved.

As we approach their exiles, I've had many clients say (with anger or shame) some version of the following to me: "I don't know what you're doing to me. I've been sober for ten years and I went out and got drunk last night." My standard reply is, "That's great, because now we have a direct line to a part we haven't healed yet." Needless to say, the perspective that symptoms are the activities of parts has been a tough sell in the psychotherapy field.

With Mona we met what I suspect were three firefighters: the sleepy dissociating one, the manic one, and the suicidal one. We also encountered one manager—the one who blamed her for what happened. How can you tell the difference? It's not about the protective activity, because virtually any activity can be used by both. For example, let's say I have a client who's a binge drinker. If he ever feels slighted, he goes to a bar and gets drunk. But over time he finds that if he stays drunk all the time, he never feels the slights in the first place. Thus, drinking has shifted from being a firefighter activity to a manager activity. The same activity is being used by different parts for different purposes—managers preempt the triggering of exiles, and firefighters react after an exile has been triggered.

Mona's example also brings up the issue of recovered memories. Mona saw herself as a naked child who is saying that the teen did something to her. Is that an accurate memory? We can't know for sure without further evidence. With IFS, however, we can retrieve and unburden that child without having to know if the memory is accurate or acting on it in the outside world, and that will still have a healing impact.

PART TWO

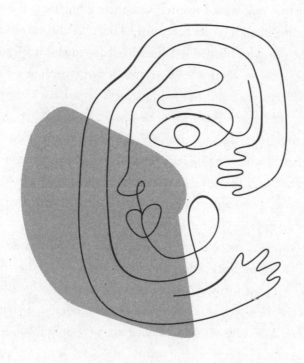

Self-Leadership

CHAPTER SIX

Healing and Transformation

What do we mean by healing and transformation in IFS? As I stated earlier, our culture (in general) and psychotherapy (specifically) have made the terrible mistake of assuming that parts are the way they seem. That is, the part that gets you to eat too much is simply a binge impulse, or the one that makes you shake in terror is just a panic attack, and that that's all they are—destructive impulses, emotions, thought patterns, or mental diseases. When you understand that you are not sick or defective and instead see that you merely have a part playing an extreme role, you'll feel relieved and comforted.

Families are like this too. For example, the literature on alcoholic families and the sibling roles kids are thrust into by the dynamics of their family often refers to the lost child, hero, and scapegoat roles. But these roles don't have anything to do with the essence of that particular child. If a good therapist came in and reorganized the family, the child would be released from their role and relax into who they really are. I'm contending that it's the same with internal families—parts are thrust into given roles and they long to be released from them. Once they are free, they transform.

If you were raised in a perfectly harmonious family in a perfectly harmonious culture, you wouldn't have parts in these roles. In fact, you would hardly notice your parts, because they would be working together, caring about each other, and feeling connected to your Self—in other words, your inner system would be in harmony. Some people do have many parts that were never burdened—parts that are still in their naturally valuable states. We therapists don't tend to work with people like this because they don't especially benefit from therapy. Instead, we usually work with the burdened parts of people that are attached to the problems they bring to us.

Recall the four goals of IFS: to liberate parts from their roles and return them to their natural states, to restore trust in the Self, to reharmonize the inner system, and to become Self-led. What we call healing in this work is crucial to achieving these goals, because burdened exiles will keep us feeling vulnerable, anxious, worthless, ashamed, lonely, and empty. And all of that will continue to drive our protectors.

Originally, the word *heal* meant "to make whole" or "to save." When we heal any level of a human system, we bring its scattered or polarized members back into harmony so as to make the system whole again. The members of healed families or companies do not disappear—instead, they reconnect and harmonize. The same is true of internal families.

An exile is healed when Self retrieves it from where it is stuck in the past.

An exile is healed when Self retrieves it from where it is stuck in the past. Then the exile can unburden and begin to reintegrate with all the other parts in the system. When that happens, the system feels far less vulnerable and protectors also feel freed up to unburden and take on new valuable roles. Thus, all the protective energy that went into keeping you from being triggered and keeping your exiles at bay is freed up for healthier endeavors and you have new access to the wonderful feelings and resources of your healed former exiles.

Here's a summary of one session with a client to illustrate: Cheryl came to see me shortly after her boyfriend had asked her to marry him. Her immediate reaction to his proposal was terror, and she couldn't understand what that was about because she really loved him. They'd been together for a long time, and she knew him very well. She was now doubting herself, thinking maybe her intuition was seeing something that she didn't. She was debating whether to pull out and was in a lot of distress about it.

I invited Cheryl to focus on that fear and get to know it. She found the terror in her gut and, when I asked how she felt toward it, she said she was very afraid of it and didn't want to hear from it. I asked her to see if those parts could give us a little space to get to know it for a few minutes. They agreed, as long as they would also have a voice afterward. Cheryl now said she was curious about the fear and asked it why it was so terrified. The fear ultimately showed her scenes of herself as a little girl when she'd felt trapped by her alcoholic father who was physically abusing her, memories she was aware of but had minimized the impact of.

It turned out that the terror was a protector who made a "never again" decision during that time—it would never again let that little girl (the exile it protected) get into that kind of position. As Cheryl listened to the fear, it began to relax, and I had her ask if we had its permission to go to the little girl and heal her. The protector said it would stay nearby and watch because it was skeptical but would let her try.

I then asked Cheryl how she felt toward that little girl. She began crying and said she felt so sorry for her. I told her to get close to the girl and show her she had that compassion for her. The girl welcomed her attention and Cheryl hugged the girl. Cheryl then asked the girl to let her know how bad it was with the father and the girl not only showed her scenes of the abuse but also had Cheryl feel the intense anxiety and betrayal that she constantly felt back then. Once that exiled little girl felt fully witnessed, Cheryl entered that time period and, while the girl watched, told the father to never touch the girl again. Then she took the girl out of that time period to the house she currently lived in and assured her that she never had to go back to that time and that Cheryl would be taking care of her now. Once she trusted that, the little girl was willing to unload all the anxiety, sense of powerlessness, and trapped feelings. The girl decided to send all that out of her and into light. She then invited a sense of safety and being lovable into her body.

Next, we invited the terror-based protector to come and see the girl to see that it didn't have to protect her anymore. The protector was impressed and happy to see that, but it wasn't quite ready to unburden its terror (protectors carry burdens, too), because it still protected other exiles that we hadn't met yet. Ultimately, we healed those exiles too. Cheryl married her boyfriend and, last I heard, they're doing fine.

So this is an example of the healing process in IFS. I present this summary here to illustrate some of what you have started experiencing in the exercises so far. With Cheryl, I quickly went to her exile. We haven't done that so far and we won't in this book. As I mentioned before, working with exiles directly can be delicate when you are by yourself. You can, however, begin to ask and learn about the exiles that are driving your protectors, and then maybe go to those exiles with the help of a trained IFS therapist or with someone who you trust can stay in Self with you and not get triggered if you show a lot of emotion.

Exiles need you to connect with them until they trust you. Then they need you to witness what happened to them and know how truly bad it was. Then you can go back to where they are stuck in the past and bring them out. At that point, they are usually willing to unburden the beliefs and emotions they've been carrying.

When you show them that they don't need to protect their exiles anymore, protectors will sometimes panic. They think you're going to downsize them. They've been at the same job for decades! I've learned to simply ask them, "What do you want to do now?" because they all have a natural desire to do something productive inside of you and, as I said earlier, you can't really predict what that's going to be. A lot of managers become advisors, so the part who's been scanning for danger constantly now wants to just be discerning and whisper to you sometimes when you go into a new situation. Others want to do the opposite of the role they've been in. The critic becomes your biggest fan. The one who kept you invisible now wants to help you shine.

Exercise: The Path

Since this part of the book is focused on Self-leadership, I want to offer you a practice to give you more of a felt sense of your Self and Self energy.

Again, get comfortable, and take deep breaths if that helps. And in your mind's eye put yourself at the base of a path. It could be one you've already been on or it could be a path that's totally new to you. And then meet with your parts at the base of this path and ask them if they'd be willing to wait there for you and let you go on this brief journey by yourself for a little while.

Notice how they react to that idea. You can try to see if those who are afraid could be comforted by those who aren't, and let them all know that you won't be gone long and this would be good for them and for you, but they don't have to let you do it if they're not ready to. It just depends on the day—some days they're okay with it and some days they're not up for it, and that's natural. If they're not up for it, then don't do it. You can spend the time just getting to know them better and understand their fears about letting you try this.

However, if they are up for it, then go ahead and head out on the path, reminding them that you'll be back soon. At different points, I'll pause and ask you to notice certain things as you go, but for now, just head out on the path.

Now I'm going to invite you to just notice what's happening as you continue on the path and, in particular, if you're thinking anything at all, because if you are thinking, that means that there's still some parts with you. See if they, too, would be willing to separate and go back with the others. If not, what's their fear?

You can also scan your body for anything that doesn't feel quite like you as your Self. If you find anything, that also is likely to be a part, and you can ask it to return to the base. If the parts you find are willing to return to the base, then you'll gradually notice yourself becoming more and more pure awareness, without a lot of thought.

And if the parts aren't willing to leave you, that's fine—you can just spend the time getting to know their fears.

If at any point you find yourself watching yourself taking this journey, that means there's a part trying to do it for you. Who is it that's watching? You can ask that part to go to the base, too, so that as you're on the path you don't see yourself—you see your surroundings in a direct, first-person sort of way.

If your parts are really trusting you to do this, then by now you should be experiencing some of the qualities we've been talking about—clarity, the absence of thought, spaciousness, present centeredness, a sense of well-being, connectedness, being in your body, confidence, and so on. You may also sense a kind of vibrating energy running through your body. We call that Self energy. If you feel that energy, invite it to run throughout your body.

If you notice any places where the energy can't flow, it's likely there is a part blocking it for some reason, so you can see if that part will go back to the base too. If you're not feeling some of these things, it means there are parts still with you, and you can scan your body and your mind to see if you can find those parts and ask if they will go back to the base.

At some point, just pause and take in this experience. Notice what it's like to have this much Self in your body. Notice the different ways you can feel it, as well as how and where Self energy manifests and reveals itself. It's important to remember these markers—that's how you can tell you're embodied. As you go through your day, you can tell how much you're there or not—how much your parts are running things.

I often check how open my heart is, whether I'm in my head thinking a lot, or if there's pressure in my shoulders and my forehead (which is where my managers hang out). If I catch any of these parts at work, I just ask them to relax and, in a sense, go back to the base and watch while I handle whatever I'm facing. "Just trust me," I tell them. Some of them need to give me some advice before they do step back, which is fine.

If by now you are feeling a lot of this Self energy, a lot of embodiment, then you have the option of inviting any messages from the universe. Maybe nothing comes, and that's okay, but people will sometimes get some clear guidance at a point like this.

Now I'm going to invite you to head back toward the base at whatever pace feels right. And when you get back to your parts, see how they react to your return and thank them for whatever risks they took to let you do this. Ask what it's been like for them. Check to see if they'll be up for letting you try it again sometime. Remind them once again that you can help them, that your goal is to earn their trust, and if any of them haven't trusted you for any reason, you're open to knowing about that and making repairs. And if you're still holding any tingling Self energy, you can extend it to your parts. You'll find that it's very healing and that you can actually direct it to your parts and to other people. I extend it to my clients when I'm working with them. If you're able to do this last piece, then just notice how your parts react to receiving the Self energy you have to offer them.

And when all that feels complete, thank your parts once again for whatever portion of this exercise they allowed and begin shifting your focus back outside. But also see if you can hold some of this Self state even as you open your eyes and come back.

Some people don't get very far down the path. For one reason or another, their parts won't allow it. Even so, it's valuable to learn why. Ask them why they don't trust that it's safe and work with their fears.

However, if parts are willing to wait at the base and let you go down the path by yourself, pretty universally people have some of the experiences I described. Self energy arises spontaneously once your parts let you be fully embodied, and you can direct that energy to yourself or others as you choose. Personally, I don't extend it to people unless I know that it's welcome, but I do encourage you to extend it to parts whether or not they have agreed to it, because they just seem to love it.

At the point where I invited you to ask for any messages, it's not uncommon that nothing happens. That being said, sometimes people do receive clear guidance about their lives or about how to work with their parts. And sometimes it's just a kind of warmth—a comforting sense they're not alone. If you do receive some information at this point, share it with your parts.

As far as where this information comes from, I don't really take a position on the issue. Whether it's your intuition, a wise part of yourself, some spirit guide, or whatever—I'll leave that up to you to discover for yourself. I'll just say that from the standpoint of empirical observation, when people are fully in Self and ask for a message, something useful often comes.

Another important aspect to this exercise is that it often forces you to notice parts that you wouldn't notice otherwise. We all have managers that are Self-like or Self-lite. We don't typically detect them, because they're so blended and involved in most of our interactions with the world. They often believe they are us, and we often believe that too. But they're just a really convincing kind of protector. They make us nice, polite, and caring, for example, but only to persuade other people to like us and think we are good. And they're often the ones responsible for keeping certain parts they don't approve of exiled. Unlike the Self, Self-like managers have protective agendas and aren't fully authentic when they convey caring, gratitude, or respect. They're what some people derogatorily refer to as the ego, but they deserve our love rather than our disdain. Just like any other protector, we need to relieve them of their huge burdens of responsibility.

Exercise: Accessing the Self Through Unblending

Like the exercise you just did, this practice will help you explore how Self operates inside of you. As you typically do to begin these exercises, take a second to get comfortable and breathe deeply, if you find that helpful. Again, we're going to check in with the parts that you are actively getting to know and just see how they're doing today. Remind them that you're there with them and that you can help them and that you care about them. You can also expand your purview to include other parts you might not know so well—just extend a recognition that you know they're there, that you care for them, and that you plan to keep getting to know them.

When you have the sense that your parts all feel at least recognized by you, ask them to relax and open up space in your mind and your body. Assure them that it will be just for a little while, and that the purpose of this exercise is to let you and them know more of who you really are.

If they are willing, again you'll notice the same experience of expanded and spacious awareness that you felt in the path exercise. This time, I want you to see if they'd be willing to let you hold this state we call Self-leadership, even when you open your eyes. So if your eyes have been closed up to now, just try opening them and see if you can feel the spaciousness. You might also find that when you open your eyes, parts jump back to attention to protect.

The practice of opening your eyes in that state is one step in a process that can lead you to experience a sense of being Self-led and embodied in your daily life. By "practice," I don't mean that Self-leadership is something you have to build up like a muscle. What we're doing in this exercise instead is just helping parts increase their trust so that they allow you to embody and lead, so that they learn to know that this is safe. The more they give it a try and see that nothing terrible happens, the more willing they'll be to keep giving it a try. More and more you can experience this other way of being and extend it to your daily life.

At the end of this practice, remember to thank your parts for all they're doing and shift your focus back outside again. And also see how much you can hold this sense of Self as you come back and go about your day.

What the Self Is and What the Self Isn't

In the early days of developing IFS, I found that when I guided clients through these exercises and their parts would open space inside, they'd spontaneously shift into Self. Furthermore, it was almost like the same person was emerging in different clients, so I began cataloging the qualities they would all manifest. And that's how I compiled the following list.

The Eight Cs of Self Energy and Self-Leadership

- Curiosity
- Calm
- Confidence
- Compassion
- Creativity
- Clarity
- Courage
- Connectedness

Although there's no sequential order to these Cs, I find that the first quality to reveal itself is often curiosity. You've probably noticed yourself becoming more curious about your parts in a new way in some of the practices you've done in this book. Compassion as a spontaneous aspect of Self blew my mind, because I'd always assumed and learned that compassion was something you had to develop. There's this idea—especially in some spiritual circles—that you have to build up the muscle of compassion over time, because it's not inherent. Again, that's the negative view on human nature at play. To be clear, what I mean by compassion is the ability to be in Self with somebody when they're really hurting and feel *for* them, but not be overwhelmed by their pain. You can only do that if you've done it within yourself. That is, if you can be with your own exiles without blending and being overwhelmed by them and instead show them compassion and help them, then you can do the same for someone in pain who's sitting across from you.

Of course, this also involves a notable degree of courage and calm. In Self, you can better handle troubling people or situations that may have paralyzed you before, and you can also go into the inner caves and abysses that once terrified you. There's confidence in doing this, and creativity as well. Once in Self, you enjoy a lot of clarity about what's going on in you and others, and this will enable you to come up with all sorts of solutions and out-of-the-box ideas.

Also, when you experience Self, you naturally feel more connected to humanity in general, and also to something larger and more encompassing—the Earth, the universe, the big SELF, or whatever your experience of this is. In other words, once in Self, you feel less isolated and lonely.

Of course, all of these qualities work together. When you get curious about a part, you naturally gain clarity regarding what it's all about, which typically results in a newfound compassion for all it's been through and is trying to do. Also, when people sense how connected they are to humanity, they feel more curious about others and have more courage to help them. In this way, even accessing one of these C qualities often leads to the appearance and activity of others. In IFS, we talk about starting with a *critical mass of Self*—enough to get the ball rolling in a good direction and the others will follow.

> When people sense how connected they are to humanity, they feel more curious about others and have more courage to help them.

That being said, it's rare for someone to be in a state of pure Self, in which all of these qualities manifest simultaneously (although the path exercise can sometimes get you fairly close). Most of the time, we're blended to some degree with different parts. But as you repeatedly prove to your parts that they don't have to blend, you gradually experience more of the eight Cs, and more often, as well. And you'll also discover other qualities rising up in you, things like joy, equanimity, forgiveness, perspective, and playfulness.

The more you're familiar with these qualities, the more you'll be able to tell when you're in Self and when you're not. I have a set of markers that I check as I go through my day, but I also find them particularly helpful during triggering times. For example, when I'm interacting with someone, I can quickly notice how open or closed my heart is and how much compassion I have for them. I'll check to see if I have a big agenda for talking to them or a tone of voice that's constrained or lacking energy. I can also just check for how many of the eight Cs I'm embodying. Different people have different markers, and I encourage you to find yours. Then you can assume that any departures from those qualities are the activities of parts, and that will enable you to identify and remind them that it's safe for them to separate and trust you to handle the situation. And when they do trust you, suddenly you'll feel your heart open more, your voice shift, your vision clear, your breathing get deeper, and so on.

It's not compassionate to passively watch suffering beings parade by.

I also want to say a little bit about what the Self isn't. Mostly I want to emphasize that the Self is not what people typically consider the ego, which in IFS terms is a cluster of managers who are trying to run your life and keep you safe. The Self also isn't your observing ego or witness consciousness, because it doesn't just passively watch. The Self isn't content to just observe. It's not compassionate to passively watch suffering beings parade by. When you really access Self, you naturally want to help your parts.

Self is not observable—you can't see your Self, because it's your seat of consciousness. It's the place from which you see your parts and the outside world. So if I asked you to hug a part of yourself and your experience was one of watching yourself performing that action, that's not your Self. As I discussed in the path exercise, if you see yourself in the inner world, it's usually a Self-like part trying to run things for you because it doesn't trust that it's safe to let you do it.

Some spiritual traditions teach that you can't really describe what the Self is, that it's somehow ineffable. I don't find that to be true. I find that when people access Self, they are characterized by the qualities we've been discussing, and they can palpably sense that they're there and other people can sense it in them. It's something quite real, as opposed to ethereal or indescribable.

The Self is indeed more than the sum of your parts. It's also in everyone, although it needs a certain amount of hardware (i.e., brain capacity) to operate fully. Young children can't fully access Self, although they can embody enough Self to heal themselves emotionally—a process witnessed and described by many IFS child therapists. Children don't have the brain power to fully protect themselves in the world, regardless of how much their parts might allow them to be Self-led. And this is partly why your parts lost trust in your Self's leadership when you were hurt as a young child—you couldn't protect them at the time, and they think they have to take over.

When you realize that you're not the insecure selfish parts that you've identified with for so long, but instead that you're this Self that's curious, calm, confident, compassionate, creative, clear, courageous, joyful, generous, and playful—and that your essence is connected to some kind of larger universal principle—you feel happy.

Spirituality and the Self

I've already discussed the kinds of spiritualities that appeal to exiles, managers, and firefighters. What about the Self? In short, the Self has an inherent desire to create and facilitate balance, harmony, wholeness, and healing at all levels of a system.

For a while now, I've been interested in the combination of IFS and psychedelic medicines, because they seem to have the effect of quickly helping protector parts relax such that people often have much more access to the Self than normal. There have been a number of research projects demonstrating the benefits of psychedelics, some of which are described in Michael Pollan's popular book, *How to Change Your Mind*.

I've been particularly interested in the use of MDMA, in part because (unlike other psychedelics) when people take MDMA they don't hallucinate or leave their bodies. Instead, they experience a sense of inner peace, joy, well-being, and a strong connection and compassion for others. In other words, they experience the same things I'd been discovering about the Self.

Notably, there's a current study (now in Phase III trials) looking into how MDMA works with patients with PTSD, and the research is being spearheaded by Michael and Annie Mithoefer—two well-trained IFS therapists. They don't practice IFS with subjects in the study unless they spontaneously begin to identify and work with a part. Instead, they just maintain a compassionate, nondirective presence and let the subjects go wherever they want. In an early study, the Mithoefers found that 70 percent of the subjects spontaneously began working with their parts in a loving way without any prompting from them.[1] This phenomenon would suggest that what happens in IFS is a natural process that we all know how to do when we are not bound up by protectors.

In general, I find that Self-led people are drawn to practices, rituals, and religious traditions that help them access more Self and feel their connection to something grander and more universal (for example, what some call God and what I refer to as SELF). They also choose spiritual paths that encourage them to bring connection, harmony, and healing to their parts, to other people, and to the planet. They frequently practice meditation, but only forms that do not denigrate or exile parts. Ideally, the meditation, mantra, chant, or mindfulness practice encourages separating from parts, soothes protectors, and allows Self to enter the body so that a person can feel the sense of well-being, calm, and love that accompanies Self embodiment.

When you access Self through meditation, it's not just a pleasant way to spend twenty minutes. You're also demonstrating to your parts that it's beneficial for them to separate because they will feel your warm presence in your body, which will reassure them and helps them trust you more. You also get a deeper felt sense of what it's like to more fully access your Self. As you go through the day, you can notice how much you are in that state or not, and if you aren't you can remind your parts to open space and let you back.

With certain kinds of meditation, you can also enter into the nondual state—that boundaryless experience of oneness in which you lose a sense of being separate and meld with something oceanic. I've had personal experience with this state both in meditation and with the psychedelic ketamine, and it's always profound. I return with a greater sense of there being much more to the universe than our senses allow us to experience, as well as increased compassion for how difficult this Earth plane can be, coupled with a commitment to make it better.

Quantum physics tells us that a photon is both a particle and a wave. I believe the same is true for the Self. Most of the time we experience Self in its particle state—we feel some degree of connectedness to others and SELF while also sensing that we are separate entities with boundaries and individual agency. Through meditation or psychedelics, however, we can lose those boundaries and enter the wave state—we become part of the much larger field of Self (SELF) in a way that feels numinous.

Actually, physics is increasingly recognizing this odd phenomenon that everything is simultaneously both particle and wave. There is a growing recognition that everything that seems solid is in fact part of a vibrating field. As leading theoretical physicist Sean Carroll says, "To understand what is going on, you actually need to give up a little bit on the notion of particles." He suggests, instead, that we think of fields. We already know about magnetic or gravitational fields, but as Carroll points out, "The universe is full of fields, and what we think of as particles are just excitations of those fields, like waves in an ocean. An electron, for example, is just an excitation of an electron field."[2]

Our parts forget our wave state of connectedness and can make us forget too.

I believe that there is a field of Self. We can enter that field through meditation, for example, and become part of that field and lose our particle-ness. We become nondual in the wave state. When the meditation is over, we particle-ize again and notice that we are in a body that is separate from everyone else. Our parts, especially when they are burdened, forget our field or wave state of connectedness and can make us forget too. As we separate from them and access purer Self, we remember our wave-state connectedness.

Because our particle Self is an aspect of a vibrating field, it will resonate with the Self in other people and in our parts. As science writer Tam Hunt writes, "All things in our universe are constantly in motion, vibrating. Even objects that appear to be stationary are in fact vibrating, oscillating, resonating, at various frequencies. Resonance is a type of motion, characterized by oscillation between two states. And ultimately all matter is just vibrations of various underlying fields. An interesting phenomenon occurs when different vibrating things/processes come into proximity: they will often start, after a little time, to vibrate together at the same frequency. They 'sync up,' sometimes in ways that can seem mysterious. This is described today as the phenomenon of spontaneous self-organization."[3]

I find that having those field or wave experiences and then remembering them helps me maintain the kind of nonattached perspective that Buddhists refer to. Not nonattached in a dissociative sense, but something nonreactive and equanimous in the face of life's slings and arrows. Rather than making me care less about what happens in this world, that kind of nonattachment actually helps me act to improve the world with less concern for my image or lifestyle. I also believe that part of the reason why psychedelics are so useful for depressed people or those at the end of their lives is that they help people hold a sense of the wave state and experience firsthand that there is much more beyond this life.

We need a balance, however, between spending time in the wave and then bringing that transcendent perspective and energy of Self to our parts and the people we encounter. Meditating can be a wonderful complement to the inner work of IFS. I have been collaborating with a couple of teachers of Tibetan Buddhism—Lama John Makransky and Lama Willa Miller—to see how some of their practices enhance the IFS process and how IFS can help them avoid spiritual bypassing and/or exiling of parts. I collaborated similarly with Loch Kelly, who's known for his way of helping people quickly get what he calls *glimpses* of Self through his adaptation of a Dzogchen Buddhist meditation.

Some have written at length on integrating IFS with Christianity.[4] I believe that the worship of Jesus and other Self-led prophets can help people access Self and inspire them to acts of altruism, as long as that worship doesn't usurp your parts' trust in your own Self. Unfortunately, there are religious denominations that do that.

My Spiritual Dawning

My father was a well-known endocrinology physician/researcher and, as such, was a scientific atheist. He was from New York (grew up in Brooklyn and Queens) and he was raised by conservative Jews who had immigrated from Hungary as teenagers. My father renounced organized religion as a young man, and he blamed it for many of the world's ills. He always proudly considered himself a Jew, but a secular Jew, not a religious one. I was highly influenced by him. My mother was raised in a Christian household on a wheat farm in Montana, and she converted to Judaism to please my father's parents. She also didn't have strong religious convictions.

Since I could never believe in the punitive, adoration-seeking, parental God I was exposed to in Judaism and Christianity, I considered myself an atheist and had little interest in anything spiritual. I tried Transcendental Meditation after college to see if it would help with my anxiety and indeed it did. Using my mantra, I could leave my troubles behind for twenty minutes, enter a thoroughly enjoyable state, and feel a warm, vibrating energy run through my body. I loved the practice but eschewed the Hindu mysticism in which it was embedded. I practiced TM regularly for years and then stopped, but I retained the memory of the wonderful state I could access.

When I first encountered Self in my clients in the early 1980s as I helped them get their parts to open space inside, I tried unsuccessfully to link the phenomenon to a psychological theory. The prevailing wisdom in developmental psychology and attachment theory was that for someone to have that kind of ego strength they had to have received *good enough* parenting as a child. To the contrary, I had clients who'd been tortured daily when they were kids, and yet they'd manifest the same undamaged Self.

I began to wonder if that Self was similar to the place TM had taken me to. I also had some students at the time who were studying various spiritual traditions. One thought the Self was like *atman* and another believed it was Buddha Nature. That encouraged me to unload my anti-religion legacy burden and search for analogues to Self in different spiritual traditions. It turns out that it was everywhere, particularly in the contemplative or esoteric sides of those traditions. Many subscribed to the belief that there is a divine essence inside everyone, and I began to consider that I had stumbled on a way to access that essence in people much more quickly than most of these traditions teach is possible.

Most of them held a goal of overcoming the ignorance of your divine nature and then becoming aware of who you really are. I was finding something similar with my clients. As people started to notice and then separate from their parts, they would have a sudden identity shift and would come to realize that they weren't their burdened parts and instead were the Self.

It seemed I had inadvertently come across a simple way to achieve what many traditions called becoming awakened.

When I say you become *awakened* by doing this work, I don't mean that you turn into a guru who lives up on a mountain somewhere and dishes out wisdom to visitors. Nor do I mean that you'll be Buddha-like all the time. What I do find is that this simple shift in the sense of who you actually are starts to pervade your life in a number of positive ways. It may not change the actual day-to-day operation of your life enormously, but it's a drastic shift in your sense of groundedness, well-being, and your sense of having a right to be here. For me, that's awakening.

The more you become familiar with it, the easier you can detect when you depart from that state—when you're having a "part attack." It stops becoming such a big deal, because you know it's temporary and that you can unblend from the part and help it out. And even if you can't unblend, you trust that your Self is still there and will return at some point. Many of our troubles come not so much from the part attack itself, but more from our panic about it, because we believe it defines us and won't end.

CHAPTER SEVEN

The Self in Action

By now you hopefully have a clear idea what the Self is and what it means to be Self-led. In this chapter, I want to take a closer look at how achieving Self-leadership affects your life both inside and outside.

Developmental psychology and attachment theory have helped us understand what children need from their caretakers as they develop. IFS can be seen as attachment theory taken inside, in the sense that the client's Self becomes the good attachment figure to their insecure or avoidant parts. I was initially amazed to discover that when I was able to help clients access their Self, they would spontaneously begin to relate to their parts in the loving way that the textbooks on attachment theory prescribed. This was true even for people who had never had good parenting in the first place. Not only would they listen to their young exiles with loving attention and hold them patiently while they cried, they would firmly but lovingly discipline the parts in the roles of inner critics or distractors. Self just knows how to be a good inner leader.

> **IFS can be seen as attachment theory taken inside.**

So why is this important? For one thing, if you can become what I call the primary caretaker of your own parts, then you free intimate partners (or therapists, children, parents, etc.) from the responsibility of taking care of raw and needy exiles. Those people then can act as the secondary caretakers of your parts, which is a much more enjoyable and feasible role.

Most of us have that reversed. Our exiles don't trust our Self and consequently they and the protectors who try to get them to calm down are looking outside of us to get what they need. When we encounter a person who resembles the profile exiles have of their ideal protector, redeemer, or lover, they feel elated, infatuated, and relieved. Through what's called positive transference, our parts put distorted images on such people, who can't help but disappoint those extreme expectations. Then comes the negative transference from angry protectors.

There are actually a number of people leading workshops on Self-led parenting. When parents are Self-led, they relate to their external children in the same way they do their internal ones—with patience, calm, clarity, love, firmness, and reassurance.

I want to briefly revisit the particle/wave view of the Self I touched on in the previous chapter. When it comes to Self in action, the main takeaway is applying some of those wave-state experiences—spaciousness, equanimity, well-being, and interconnectedness—to our day-to-day lives. With that expanded sense of awareness, we are far more likely to have compassion for others, because at some level we remember that they are us.

When we view other people as utterly separate, mono-mind beings, it's hard not to totalize them. We objectify them as a narcissist, psychopath, or racist, and miss the opportunity to connect with other parts of them. When we solidify somebody in a particular way without paying attention to their inner system of exiles and protectors, it's much, much harder to keep our heart open and act toward them in an effective way.

At the time of this writing, our president, Donald Trump, is an example of that for me. Some of my protectors can totalize him and see him as one of those diagnostic categories. And if I had the opportunity to meet him, my goal would likely be to shame him into changing, which—because of the way he reacts to attempts to shame him—would totally backfire. But I could do something different entirely. If instead I adopted the perspective of multiplicity inherent in IFS, then I could see behind his protectors and know that they're just trying to keep him safe and make him feel better. They themselves are trying to deal with the exiles in him that make him feel so worthless, and no doubt they are all stuck in horrible places in his childhood. This different approach is like good parenting too—I can have compassion for the man while still feeling upset at the damage his protectors are doing and working to stop them.

For a few years now, I've been training social activists to lead from Self. In my experience, many people are called to become activists because they were badly hurt in the past, carry lots of exiles, and consequently have protectors who don't want anyone else to suffer the way they did. As a result, their activism is sometimes protector-led, which can further polarize issues and alienate potential allies. That's certainly understandable, but I think we can do better. As Charles Eisenstein observes, "We see again and again, within environmental organizations, within leftist political groups, the same bullying of underlings, the same power grabs, the same egoic rivalries as we see everywhere else. If these are played out in our organizations, how can we hope that they won't be played out in the world we create, should we be victorious?"[1]

This goes for me, as well. Although we aspire to be Self-led at the IFS Institute, we certainly have our own blind spots, and—since I'm the leader—many of them reflect my own burdened parts. My growing awareness of this dynamic has inspired me to commit to steadily working on myself, as do the members of my training and administrative staff.

Session Three: Ethan and Sarah

I include this next transcript because it illustrates work with social activists. It also clearly demonstrates many aspects of IFS related to spirituality and the Self, which we have only talked about so far.

Ethan and Sarah Hughes (their real names) are leaders in the living-off-the-grid movement. They embrace a very simple life on a small homestead, living without electricity, using candles at night. They cook and heat their home with a wood stove, keep food cool in a root cellar, and travel via bicycle and public transportation instead of by car. They deliberately live below the poverty line so as to not have to pay income tax—or, as Ethan puts it, *war tax*. They welcome over 1,500 visitors per year who come to get inspired and learn how they do it. In this way, Ethan and Sarah are modeling how it's possible to step away from the frantic, driven pace of our lives and access other parts of ourselves. When people stay with the Hughes family, they are often amazed at how quickly they come to enjoy this sustainable lifestyle that respects and keeps them connected to the Earth.

Ethan and Sarah had been learning about IFS, but hadn't tried it yet. This was my first encounter with them.

ETHAN: I think one of the issues that recurs is that this part that I call the *destroyer of injustice* will attack anything, including Sarah, that it perceives to be supporting white supremacy or classism. An example is that we live as a family of four in a house of 500 square feet and Sarah wants an addition. I tell her we've got to live smaller and there's homeless people, but it comes out in a way that creates a lot of disharmony or far worse.

DICK: And how often would you say that comes out?

E: We almost separated two years ago and since then I pulled it back a lot.

SARAH: Yes, we've both pulled back. And when it happens, we don't talk about it. But the IFS framework is super helpful for us to understand what is happening, we didn't have that tool before.

D: So Sarah, when you sniff the presence of that part of Ethan, what happens inside of you?

S: I have some anger that comes up, but that hasn't been safe for me, so I have to silence it. There's a silencer part. So I have this silent anger. And I've also had a dissociative part that can pull me away or can help me forget about our conflict so that I can open up to him again. Because I have a really tender heart and I like to be open. So when his destroyer part comes out, I then go [*makes gasping sound*] like that. I clamp up in my throat.

D: Okay, well you guys are well ahead of the game in that you already know who the inner players are. So, Ethan, you've got this destroyer of injustice. When Sarah reacts to it like that, what happens inside of you?

E: I feel really sad because it feels like this part of me has no space, so I start to think that I shouldn't be with Sarah. That she's too tender-hearted for this fiery warrior. I feel like I'm hurting someone I love so much. So I have to shut it out.

D: You feel like you shouldn't be with Sarah because you see the damage it does. And you don't want to keep inflicting that.

E: But I also don't want to shut it down.

D: You want that part to have space.

E: So it's been a dance, sometimes a brawl. I want to say I'm sorry.

D: Okay, let's do that. Let's see what kind of repair we can do right now. Are you open to that Sarah? [*She nods*]

S: Go ahead, Ethan.

E: [*Sobbing*]

D: That's good, stay with that sadness. That's great.

E: [*Still sobbing*] What's coming up is that I know how much you love the world. How much you cry because the monarchs are dying. You cried when the tree frog got extinct. I'm so sorry. There's like these two sides of this part—it's trying to protect the world for you and then hurting you. This all feels so sacred, and I've been trying for so many years . . .

D: That's great, let me pause you for a little bit. Sarah, how was it to hear that?

S: I felt especially touched when you said that you want to protect me because you know I love everything so much.

D: So you get it that that's the intention of that part.

S: Yeah, I know that part. It has sometimes been damaging, but it's also one of the reasons I love him.

D: So my inclination is to do a piece of work with that destroyer part. Are you up for that, Ethan?

E: Yeah.

D: So while we do this, it's important that you, Sarah, stay in Self. Okay, so are you ready?

E: Yeah.

D: So find that guy in or around your body. The destroyer of injustice. Where do you feel him?

E: Right here [*points to his chest*].

D: And as you notice him, how do you feel toward him?

E: I'm both grateful and afraid.

D: Let's get the one who's afraid to give us the space to get to know him. That part can go into a separate room—it doesn't need to be a part of this. It can trust you and me to help the destroyer part.

E: Yeah, is it okay to ask the scared part to step aside and witness?

D: Yes, totally. Now how do you feel toward this guy?

E: What's coming up is that I want it to have a place of power in a world that needs it, but in a way that doesn't put people off or scare them.

D: That's right. Let him know that that's your intention. And that you do value him and feel gratitude toward him. And just see how he reacts.

E: He doesn't fully believe me because I've shut him down so many times.

D: Yeah, so let him know that you can understand that it's hard for him to trust what you're saying. Because you did shut him down. That makes sense, doesn't it, that he would have trouble trusting you?

E: Yeah.

D: So we're just going to work on repairing your relationship with him in a similar way to which you just did with Sarah. See what he needs to start to trust you again.

E: He's saying he's committed to keeping me from falling asleep. He needs to trust that I'm remembering to stay committed to real justice for all life.

D: Okay, so what do you say to him about all that?

E: I think he's right, but I have been isolated so often by his choices that have been driven by love, but then trigger people—my attempts just bring up other parts in other people. He's right that there are other parts that want to go to sleep for a while—that are scared of not belonging.

D: So we have that polarization happening inside. All right, so let it know that there are those parts that aren't thrilled that he can do that to people. So you can understand why it's hard for him to trust you.

E: [*Sobbing*] He's saying how much he knows that I love the ocean and he doesn't want me to have to explain to my daughters why there aren't any fish left in the ocean.

D: Yeah, so just let him know that we get how much he cares and how much he really, really wants things to change and improve. How committed he is to that. How we really admire that. How's he doing, how's he reacting?

E: He's feeling excited that he could come out. And he says he's excited to work with me.

D: Good. That's exactly what we're trying to do, to make it so that he doesn't have to take over all the time and, instead, can work with you and maybe have you speak for him. And see if that sounds okay to him.

E: Yeah. He's seeing ripples of potential from that. He keeps coming up in images, and he's saying, "What the fuck are we doing? Let's all go cook so that the cooking staff in this retreat center, that are mainly marginalized people of color, can come in and get this work."

D: It's hard for him to even indulge in this. Ask him, Ethan, if he protects other parts of you, if he's willing to disclose that.

E: There's a part that just cries, curled up in a ball all day, and doesn't even move.

D: Yeah, so ask him, if we could go to that part and heal it so it wasn't feeling that anymore and it felt good, would he be able to relax a little more? We're not asking him to change his role at all—we're asking if he'd be willing to relax a little more and trust you more to speak for him.

E: He's just saying that the last time I got close to that part I cried for a month—for four hours a night—and he says there is no room for me crying when everything is dying.

D: So tell him if he gives us permission, that's not going to be the outcome. Instead, we're going to go to that guy, without being overwhelmed by him, and we're going to get him out of where he's stuck back there. We're going to unload a lot of the sadness that he carries. See how that appeals to this destroyer guy.

E: He's okay to try it.

D: We really appreciate that. And before we go there, see if there are any other parts that are afraid to let us go to that guy.

E: The other parts seem excited.

D: Good. That's great. Are you ready?

E: Yeah.

D: So focus on that guy curled in a ball, find him in your body or around your body. And how do you feel toward him as you notice him there?

E: I'm so sorry he has to come into a world like this.

D: That's right, so let him know that. That the world is so bad. That he had no choice about it. And see how he reacts to your compassion.

E: He looked up for a moment out of the ball.

D: Good. And how close are you to him in terms of feet away.

E: About five feet.

D: Okay, good. So right now, we're just going to extend this compassion to him, until he starts to trust that he's not alone anymore. That you're there.

E: He says he can't go on without his dad.

D: Without his dad? So let him know we get how much he needs his dad. Just let him know you get that. But also, if it feels sincere, if it feels right, let him know that you can be a dad to him if he likes that.

E: He stopped crying.

D: Good. You still about five feet away?

E: I'm kneeling down a little closer.

D: Good. That's really good. So we're just going to keep going this way, until he trusts you as someone who can take care of him like a dad.

E: I'm holding him now.

D: Good. How's he reacting?

E: He's crying again a little bit.

D: Let him know it's fine to cry while you hold him. Is it okay to feel some of his feelings right now?

E: [*Sobbing*] Yes.

D: That's really great. Let him know you get that, that he carries an enormous amount of sadness.

E: He's hugging me so tight.

D: He's hugging you so tight?

E: Yeah.

D: That's great. Are you ready to ask him what he needs you to know about what happened to him?

E: Yes.

D: So ask him to really let you feel and see and sense so that you can feel all this sadness and how bad it was.

E: He feels so misunderstood.

D: Feels so misunderstood. By you or by other people?

E: Other people.

D: Yeah, so tell him to show that to you. What happened to make him feel so misunderstood.

E: [*Sobbing*] He says, "Why is everyone drinking and driving and killing people?" He says that it's so fucked up.

D: Yeah, that is fucked up. Let him know that it's a really good question.

E: He says his mom and brother didn't understand.

D: He says his mom and brother didn't understand. Didn't understand him, or what?

E: He's saying how fucked up it is that people do that.

S: His father was hit by a drunk driver.

D: Yeah, I was guessing that. And how old was this boy, Ethan?

E: Thirteen.

D: Yeah, okay. All right. So tell him to go on, this is really good. That he can let you see and sense and feel all of it. Just tell him to keep going, whatever he needs you to get.

E: I'm just sad that no one could teach me how to be with him.

D: Yeah, so tell him you're really sorry you haven't been able to be with him in this way. All these years. Let him know you're sorry. That he kind of had to be locked up in there.

E: He's relaxing in there a little bit.

D: That's great.

E: He's thirteen, but he's small.

D: Yeah. Ask him if you get it now, how bad it was for him. If there's more.

E: He's saying how hard it was to go to public high school. [*Sobbing*] That after the devastation everyone was talking about what they're wearing. The teachers didn't even talk to him.

D: Teachers didn't talk to him.

E: Like nothing happened. It's like he was in fucking prison.

D: That's right.

E: He hated going to the fucking mall.

D: So let him know you're getting all this too.

E: There's one more piece, where there's a part of him that felt like he's partly responsible.

D: For the accident.

E: Yeah.

D: Ask him why.

E: Because his dad asked him to go to the basketball game the night he was hit. He chose to go to the arcade with some other people.

D: So if he had gone with the dad, the accident wouldn't have happened, or what? What's the logic there?

E: All that I'm hearing is that superficiality kills.

D: Got it, okay. Does this make sense that he would believe that?

E: [*Nods in agreement*]

D: Let him know you get that. So he's been anti-superficiality ever since. That makes sense. That makes a lot of sense. So, Ethan, what do you say to him about whether it was his fault?

E: I tell him it wasn't.

D: Yeah. We need to stay with that until he starts to believe it. How's he reacting to you saying that?

E: He's apologizing that he got caught up in the superficiality of the culture.

D: He's apologizing. I'm not quite following that.

E: That's what came up, he's sorry that he got caught up in that. It was the first time my dad had invited me. He was the middle school basketball coach, and it was the first time he had invited me to come to a game.

D: He chose the superficial thing instead.

E: Yeah, so he wanted me to go to the game, and other people were saying, "Let's go to the arcade instead." And I got caught up in the culture.

D: Yeah, so let him know you get that. Let him know you get why he feels so guilty about that. [*Pause*] How's he doing now?

E: He's calm again.

D: Good. Just see if he feels like you get everything he wants you to get.

E: He's nodding yes.

D: Okay, good. So, Ethan, I want you to go back into that time period and be with him the way he needed somebody and tell me when you're there with him.

E: I see myself stepping in front of the bed, and he's crying, so there's someone else that's there, and I'm watching him.

D: You see yourself there? So ask that part that's trying to do it for you to let you do it, such that you don't see yourself—you're just there with him. Just tell me when you're in there with him.

E: Okay.

D: How are you being with him?

E: He's crying a bit and I have my hands on his feet.

D: Perfect. Stay with him that way.

E: [*Pause, breathing*]

D: Can he tell that you're there?

E: Yeah.

D: Is he glad?

E: Yeah.

D: Okay, good. Now ask if there's anything he wants you to do with him or for him before we take him to a good, safe place.

E: He just wants me to hold him.

D: Go ahead and hold him.

E: And he wants me to tell him that it's going to be okay.

D: Okay, go ahead and do both of those things.

E: [*Pause, sniffling*] It's switching between me holding him, and me watching me holding him.

D: So that guy, just be firm with him. We get he's trying to help. Just let him know you don't need that, that you can handle this.

E: Okay.

D: [*Pause*] How's he doing with you now?

E: He says he doesn't want to be alone.

D: Good. Ask him if there's anything else he wants you to do with him or for him back there, before we take him to a good place. Did he need you to talk to the family for him?

E: He's just saying that he's asking where my mom is, that he's all alone and it's late.

D: Yeah. Does he want you to get her or does he just want you to explain it?

E: Yeah, I'm telling him right now, because Mom wasn't there very much, and she had to work.

D: Okay.

E: He's asking why the neighbors didn't come by.

D: What are you saying?

E: They have their own challenges.

D: Let him know that he should have had somebody, that he deserved to.

E: [*Pause*]

D: And that he has you now.

E: He's smiling for the first time.

D: Great. Okay. Just see if he's ready now and we'll go someplace he'll like

E: Yeah.

D: So where would he like to go? It could be the present or it could be a fantasy place.

E: He wants to swim in the ocean.

D: Good. Let's take him to the ocean. And before he swims, though, tell him he never has to go back there, and that you're going to be taking care of him. And ask him if he's ready to unload the feelings and beliefs he got back then.

E: He's just asking, he's saying he wants a lot of turtles and seaweed and dolphins. He wants the ocean as it was before.

D: Okay, so let's set that up for him.

E: He's happy to see so much life.

D: That's great. And then ask him again if he's ready to unload this stuff.

E: Yeah.

D: Where does he carry it in his body? In or around his body?

E: Back of his head.

D: What would he like to give it up to? Light, water, fire, wind, earth, or anything else.

E: Water.

D: Yeah, so tell him to let that all out of the back of his head and let the ocean take it.

E: He let some of it go, but some of it he doesn't want to forget.

D: Okay. So he wants to hold on to the memories?

E: He said he could put them in a canoe.

D: So he'll put them in a canoe. Let's do that. Let's put it out of the back of his head and into the canoe.

E: He realizes there's more in his heart and in his stomach.

D: Yeah, let's get that out too. No need to carry any of this stuff anymore.

E: [*Pause*] He's floating.

D: That's great. That's great.

E: He's pushing the canoe away.

D: That's great. Great. How's he feeling now?

E: He's smiling and not crying but still feeling some sadness.

D: And is that sadness something he wants to unload, or something he wants to express to you?

E: He wants to unload it.

D: Okay. To the ocean also or the canoe?

E: To the ocean. He wants my dad.

D: Ethan, there is one thing we could do with that. You can invite your dad's spirit to come and he may or may not come. But you can see if he wants to invite your dad's spirit to come.

E: He does.

D: Okay, so tell him to do it. And we'll see if your dad's spirit shows up.

E: He's here.

D: That's good. That's great. And let's just see if there's something he wants this boy to know. If the boy wants to ask him anything.

E: He's smiling and the boy is just happy to see him. He's in a rowboat and he's just smiling.

D: Good. So does the boy want to give him that sadness? Or what does the boy want to do with that sadness?

E: The boy is asking my dad if he gives him that sadness will he lose the connection.

D: And what does your dad say?

E: He says, "I'm right here all the time."

D: Yeah. And how's that for the boy to hear?

E: He's climbed into the rowboat with my dad [*sobbing*]. He likes being held by my dad.

D: Great. Really, really good.

E: He's now put a hand out and he's calling me.

D: Good.

E: He's calling me over.

D: Yeah, so you can come over there too.

E: [*Sobbing and breathing deeply*] I'm holding the boy now, my dad is watching and he's smiling.

D: Good, Ethan. Let's invite the original guy, the destroyer of injustice, to come in and see this boy. Just see how he reacts.

E: There are more parts there and they're happy to see him.

D: That's great.

E: One of them is dancing. [*Breathing*] The destroyer isn't dancing but he's kind of smiling and nodding. His arms are crossed [*laughter*].

D: Good.

E: I think he's a little impatient.

D: I get that to him what we are doing is indulgent.

E: He's kind of smiling and laughing with me now.

D: You can ask him if he'd like to unload anything that he carries that doesn't belong to him.

E: Yeah, a burden.

D: Where does he carry it on his body, in his body?

E: Neck and back.

D: Do you know what it is?

E: That protecting life is up to him.

D: Yeah, that's right. What would he like to give it up to?

E: I saw an image of a huge mountain, like half mountain, half woman.

D: Tell him to give up what is in his neck and back to this mountain woman.

E: He's kneeling down and putting it down like a sacred sword.

D: Good.

E: He's looking up just to make sure it's the right thing to do for her.

D: What does she say?

E: It's nonverbal, but it's a yes.

D: Good.

E: He wants to grab the sword, but he really wants me to know that he wants to be doing something for light.

D: Yeah, let him know you guys can figure that out, that you may not need to do it now. How does he feel without the sword?

E: A lot lighter, but he wants purpose.

D: Like, what am I going to do?

E: Yeah, wanting to hold something.

D: In the absence of a sword, Ethan, tell him he can invite whatever he wants inside his body, including purpose, and just see if something comes in.

E: Goddess mountain gives a ball of light that he is holding.

D: Good, that's great. How's he like holding that ball of light?

E: It's glowing.

D: Good, that's great.

E: He's smiling. He doesn't want it to stop.

D: Yeah, so tell him it doesn't have to stop. He can just hold it. Does that feel complete for now?

E: I guess [*laughing*]. I'd just like to connect with you [*to Sarah*] somehow.

D: Feel free.

S: Do you want me to come to you?

E: It would be great if you could sit on my lap [*sobbing*].

S: [*Sits on his lap stroking his head*]

This session illustrates many of the ideas and processes we've been talking about so far, as well as some phenomena we haven't explored yet. Let me start by issuing two caveats: First, not all sessions go so well. Ethan and Sarah had a head start in that they'd been playing with IFS for some time, had gotten to know key parts, and were both taking responsibility for their own role in the conflict. Also, Ethan's parts already trusted his Self enough to step back when we asked them to, and that's often not the case initially. Second, I encouraged Ethan to go to his exile—the crying boy curled in a ball—and, as I've stressed before, I encourage you to not do that without help. I include this session here just to let you know what's possible—not to model what you should be doing.

Here's a reflection Ethan shared with me later on: "From the moment the unburdening occurred, I noticed a greater spaciousness in my being when issues of justice presented themselves. The fire for justice and the end of suffering still burned fiercely, but that fire was shared with others instead of burning against others. The shift was one of power *over* (I see injustice and you don't see it. Now I will show you!) to power *with* (I see injustice and you do not see it. Now I will be gentle and curious with you to help you see it or discern together if injustice is actually occurring). I have become more effective in navigating these situations because of the openness. It feels like before the unburdening, my fire for justice was in a small room and people got dragged into the room and were very uncomfortable (hot, burned, suffocated), and now, after unburdening, the fire is outside in expansiveness and vastness around it. People are invited to sit by the fire. It becomes a life-giving campfire and people can freely choose the distance from the fire they need to be comfortable. I can see clearly this is what my Self wants. Upon returning home, the energetic field around my body was shifted due to the unburdening. New people and opportunities were drawn into my life such as working with indigenous women to form a community and being invited to more deeply support the queer and trans community in Maine. My energy around justice work is now more grounded and clean, which I believe the people from oppressed positions and communities could sense."[2]

Because so much happened in this session, I want to highlight a few aspects. The beginning illustrates how IFS couple therapy often goes. We ask about the parts of each partner that get into it with the other and, when it's clear that transforming one partner's part will produce a big change, we ask to start with that one. If it were ongoing couples therapy, we would likely work with Sarah's parts in the next session.

Our transition to working with Ethan's destroyer of injustice illustrates many things I covered in the previous pages, namely that this is the kind of protector I find dominating many social activists. It's crucial to ask protectors' permission to heal what they protect (that is, by honoring their work and without expecting or asking them to change). We reassure parts that it's safe to let us go to those places.

There are certain steps to healing an exile—in this case, having Ethan's Self form a trusting relationship with the thirteen-year-old boy, witness what happened to him in that past time and the burdens he accrued (for example, his beliefs about his responsibility and hatred of superficiality), retrieve the boy from the past and help him unburden, and then bring in the protectors so they see they don't have to do their jobs anymore.

And then there's the more spiritual aspects I hinted at, here involving the spirit of Ethan's dad. In my work, I've had many experiences with clients in which the image of a dead relative comes spontaneously at a moment like the one Ethan experienced, and that presence has a salubrious effect. I've learned to ask clients if they are interested in inviting such a visit if they've accessed a lot of Self and it feels like it might be helpful. Most of the time the figure's image does arrive like this and—unlike when they were alive—they seem to be quite unburdened and in Self, as was the case with Ethan's father.

What is this phenomenon? Is it the client's imagination, or another part playing the role of the dead father? Or is it actually the father's spirit? I don't pretend to know the answer. I'm an empiricist in the sense that I endeavor to study these phenomena without presumption. My father was a good scientist and one of his most important messages to me was to follow the data even if it takes you far outside your paradigm. This IFS adventure has done that over and over, and these experiences in which dead relatives show up illustrates that. I'm also a pragmatist, so if these visits seem to help, I go with it. In my experience, this phenomenon seems to help clients a great deal.

Later in the session, as Ethan goes to unburden his protector, he spontaneously sees an image of a being that's half mountain and half woman—a figure he calls a mountain goddess. She gives the protector a ball of light when he asks for purpose. What is this? This is another phenomenon that occurs spontaneously in many clients. At crucial points, what people refer to as guides will come and help them. I don't pretend to know what this is all about, either. That is some of the adventure of this work—you never know what you and your client will encounter in their inner world. The key is to stay curious and to see if whatever comes seems to be helping or not.

I want to add that these seemingly mystical experiences don't only happen in people who already believe in such things. I've worked with total atheists and clients whose religious beliefs preclude such things, and many of them at first react with anger or fear.

I sometimes think about the people referred to as shamans—people who regularly work with ancestral spirits as well as entities comparable to Ethan's mountain goddess. Some believe that an alternative universe or realm exists that we can access with various practices—drumming, chanting, dance, prayer, ingesting hallucinogenic plants, hyperventilation, sleep deprivation, dreaming, fasting, rituals, and so on. Could it be that by simply focusing on our parts, we can enter that same realm?

Becoming Self-Led

Ideally, Ethan's destroyer of injustice will feel less compelled to take over in the angry and judgmental way that it had before. Instead, it will trust Ethan's Self to speak and act for it, and take on more of an advisor role. It will retain its passion for justice and love for people and the Earth, but will rely on Ethan's courage, clarity, confidence, compassion, and so on to effectively express its beliefs and pursue its goals.

In addition to those eight C-words describing the Self, I've also identified five that begin with a P: patience, persistence, presence, perspective, and playfulness. Self-led social activists are able to draw upon these qualities, as well. Because the Self can maintain a long-range perspective, you can be patiently persistent in your efforts, without the highly attached urgency that tends to polarize. With the IFS perspective, you also avoid the mono-mind thinking that makes people pigeonhole each other and, instead, you can see past your opponents' protectors to the exiles that drive their extremes and have compassion for them. When you are present in Self, you can be highly forceful without escalating conflicts, because the other doesn't feel denigrated.

Leading from Self amid conflict becomes a goal unto itself. For example, when I have a fight with my wife, I ask my parts to step back and let me stay to relate to her, and not simply to get her to calm down and be nicer (although it often has that impact). Instead, I do this to further convince my parts that I can lead my system. So the goal becomes trying to maintain the presence of Self regardless of how the other is behaving.

To do this, it helps when your parts come to realize that you are not a child anymore and that, as your Self, you possess powerful qualities and can be forcefully assertive when necessary. Often protectors look down on some of these qualities. For example, they think you're a mushy bundle of passive compassion with porous boundaries who will give away the farm. Or that you are too innocent, trusting, or scared to take care of them. They only know you as you are when you blend with those other parts. It's often shocking to your protectors to discover that you are able to separate from those parts, and they learn that you have agency and can protect your system, so they don't have to.

This is quite a challenge in some circumstances—when you face threatening people or events, for example. And yet, amid the terror or the rage, the Self in each of us is always there—the *I* in the storm, the calm depth beneath the roiling waves. There is always Self. No matter how triggered and extreme our parts, if we can get them to separate enough, we'll have access to at least some of the qualities of the Self, and we'll be able to be with our fear or anger, rather than blend with it.

I'm reminded of an episode in my life several years ago when my wife, Jeanne, and I were visiting my brother and sister-in-law at their place in Hawaii. It was a day of very high surf and despite Jeanne's warnings, I decided to wade into the shallows, assuming I was safe if the water didn't get past my thighs. I unknowingly took a step off a drop-off and was suddenly in the middle of a riptide pulling me quickly out to sea. Not knowing any better, I tried to swim directly back to shore and got nowhere. I tried to rest by rolling on my back, but the waves washed into my mouth, and I started choking.

As I became increasingly fatigued, it began to dawn on me that I might not make it. Parts of me began screaming repeatedly in my head, "We're going to die!" I was able to separate from them enough to let them feel me saying, "We might die, but I'll be with you as we do," and I sensed them calm down. Just when I was ready to give up, my sister-in-law arrived at the beach, saw me struggling, and pointed frantically for me to swim horizontally, toward the huge waves. It was counterintuitive, but exactly what I needed to do to get back to shore. With no energy to spare, I gave it one last go, and I was eventually carried in by the waves. I learned later that a man had drowned in that same spot days earlier, so I felt extremely lucky.

The point of sharing this story is that even in the face of real danger, it's possible to hold your parts. Sure, it's difficult. I've had years of experience showing my parts that things go better when they separate and let me handle things, so they trusted me enough to do that. But any measure of Self-leadership is helpful in dire circumstances. It may not lead to the kind of life-saving luck I had, but it's always better to face your challenges from a place of calm, courage, clarity, and confidence, rather than from scared, dissociating, or impulsive parts. The more Self we bring to the crises we encounter (for example, the current pandemic), the more likely its lessons will be learned at all levels—planetary, national, and individual.

Even in the face of real danger, it's possible to hold your parts.

CHAPTER EIGHT

Vision and Purpose

Generally speaking, as you get more access to Self and become more Self-led, you also attain more clarity about the vision you have for your life, which means that your priorities may be quite different than they were when your protectors were in charge. When we have lots of exiles, our protectors have no choice but to be egotistic, hedonistic, or dissociative. Even those who seem selfless because they give so much to others are often more concerned about being viewed by others as virtuous (or not being punished by God). Your protectors' goals for your life revolve around keeping you away from all that pain, shame, loneliness, and fear, and they use a wide array of tools to meet those goals—achievements, substances, food, entertainment, shopping, sex, obsession with your appearance, caretaking, meditation, money, and so on. Your protectors work tirelessly and valiantly to keep pumping air into your ego so it doesn't deflate and sink in the abyss of exiled emotion.

> When we have lots of exiles, our protectors have no choice but to be egotistic, hedonistic, or dissociative.

As the urges of these protectors consume most of your attention, they drown out and keep exiled the more sensitive and loving parts of you. As you unburden your exiles, it allows your protectors to transform, and you begin hearing more from those parts of you that aren't so obsessed and driven—the ones who love being truly intimate with others, the ones who want to create art and move your body, the ones who want to play with family and friends, and the ones who just love being in nature. When you're more Self-led, you become a more complete, integrated, and whole person.

This is what healing means in IFS—wholeness and reconnection, and a Self who wants to facilitate that at all levels of a system. As Wendell Berry writes, "Healing complicates the system by opening and restoring connections among the various parts, in this way restoring the ultimate simplicity of their union. . . . The parts are healthy insofar as they are joined harmoniously to the whole. . . . Only by restoring the broken connections can we be healed. Connection is health."[1]

In addition to connecting to neglected parts, as you access more Self you shift from being led by your parts' desires to being led by your heart's desires. That is, you begin getting inklings of a different vision for your life's journey that brings more meaning to it. While there are countless approaches out there that coach you to articulate and pursue a meaningful vision for your life, too often those attempts come from your managers rather than your Self. In my experience, it's best to wait until your protectors have relaxed so that the vision emerges—in this way, you receive your vision rather than create it.

When people access Self, they often quickly sense their purpose.

A number of spiritual traditions teach that we each have a true path or calling, and part of why we're here in this life is to find out and fulfill what that is. Jean Houston uses a term borrowed from Aristotle to describe this—*entelechy*: "the seeded, coded essence in you which contains both the patterns and possibilities for your life."[2] Christians sometimes refer to Ephesians 2:10, which states that God created each of us for a specific purpose.

When parts unburden, they often immediately sense their original purpose and take on a commensurate new role. When people access Self, they often quickly sense their purpose. In the outer world, that realization might take years; in the inner world, it often happens immediately.

Humanistic psychologist Abraham Maslow is well known for his ideas on *self-actualization*. He asserted that after our basic needs for safety, belonging, and affection are met, we become aware of a higher need to do what we're best suited for. "A musician must make music, an artist must paint, a poet must write, if he is to be ultimately at peace with himself. . . . This tendency might be phrased as the desire to become more and more what one idiosyncratically is, to become everything that one is capable of becoming."[3] I find there to be too much striving in Maslow's early writings to "be all you can be," but I agree that our purpose or vision naturally arises when our survivalist parts relax. After Maslow had studied self-actualizing people later in his life, he found that while they may not have maximized their potential in every area of their lives, these people worked at causes that benefited others and were precious to them, such that it didn't feel like work at all. Through their Self-led vision, they had found their purpose and, consequently, their lives felt full of meaning.

As psychologist Scott Barry Kaufman notes, "Creative self-actualizers are capable of transcending the ordinary dichotomy between the intelligence of the mind and the wisdom of the heart. They are able to throw their whole selves into their work, flexibly switching between seemingly contradictory modes of being—the rational and the irrational, the emotional and the logical, the deliberate and the intuitive, and the imaginative and the abstract—without prejudging the value of any of these processes."[4] This is an excellent description of the flexible integration that occurs in a Self-led system. The different parts maintain their separateness while communicating and collaborating with each other, while the Self conducts this inner orchestra.

Different parts maintain their separateness while communicating and collaborating with each other, while the Self conducts this inner orchestra.

Well-known neuropsychiatrist Dan Siegel has emphasized the importance of such integration in healing and has described IFS as a good way to achieve that. He writes, "Health comes from integration. It's that simple, and that important. A system that is integrated is in a flow of harmony. Just as in a choir, with each singer's voice both differentiated from the other singers' voices but also linked, harmony emerges with integration. What is important to note is that this linkage does not remove the differences, as in the notion of blending: instead it maintains these unique contributions as it links them together. Integration is more like a fruit salad than a smoothie."[5] This, again, is one of the basic goals of IFS. Each part is honored for its unique qualities while also working in harmony with all the others.

In contrast, in a protector-led system, either one coalition of parts dominates so much that you lose access to the resources of the others, or it's just internal chaos and conflict in which parts constantly interrupt and sabotage one another, because there's no steady leadership.

Life Changes and Backlash

When you begin getting glimpses of a Self-led vision, it's common for parts to react homeostatically. The grander your vision, the bigger their backlash. "Don't kid yourself," they'll say, "Who do you think you are that you could do that!" Or "What's the point—everything's so screwed up that it will never make any difference!" Or the ever-popular "You can't make a living doing that!"

When I first got the vision of IFS and considered devoting my life to it, I had all of those reactions and more. After receiving my vision, I had to work with my parts just to manifest the initial stages, and my parts backlashed each step of the way. This book represents a bolder step on the journey of trying to bring IFS to a much wider audience, and here those voices are again—right on cue. The difference now is that these parts trust my leadership, so they aren't as loud or harsh as they once were, and they respond well to my reassurances. They know that if some of you don't like this book and even attack it for some reason, we'll be okay, because I will take care of them. That's the kind of work that will allow you to pursue your own vision. Bring all of your parts along for the ride—no need to exile or override the dissenters.

Fair warning: I've had clients quit lucrative careers to pursue what had only been a faint inner yearning throughout their lives. Recently, a high-powered corporate lawyer left his firm and went back to school to become a gym teacher. This was not something I led him to, but as this client healed, he finally listened and had the courage to act. Such a move takes much more courage than it used to. These days, people can hardly earn a living doing the most meaningful kinds of work, whereas some of the most meaningless kinds are the highest paid. That being said, Self-led people do have less need for material things, and that helps a lot. Some, like my lawyer client, are willing and better able to take the hit, but it's a shame that they have to.

Not all of my increasingly Self-led clients quit their jobs or make U-turns in their careers, but they typically change their lives in some way for the better. Many get involved in creative or altruistic activities that are rewarding in their own right and provide a new sense of meaning. Self-led visions are frequently based on an increased sense of connection to humanity and the Earth, and people begin embodying the desire to help both. In addition, when you are Self-led, these activities are more satisfying, because you are actually present in your body while you are experiencing them, versus a life of impatiently planning the next activity or obsessing about how you could be doing something more productive or pleasurable. When Self-led, you actually can live in the present because you no longer have so many parts that are hurting and stuck in the past; you are no longer trying to protect them by worrying about or planning the future.

Interestingly enough, you might even have parts who tell you your vision is too small! But as Charles Eisenstein reports, "So many people squelch the expression of their gifts by thinking that they must do something big with them. One's own actions are not enough—one must write a book that reaches millions. How quickly this turns into a competition over whose ideas get heard. How it invalidates the small, beautiful strivings of the bulk of humanity—invalidates, paradoxically, the very things we must start doing en masse to sustain a livable planet."[6]

As people become more Self-led, they find themselves acting altruistically without effort and without so much inner debate, because it just feels natural to them to want to help others. This is because Self recognizes that you and the others are part of a larger body of humanity. It's the same as when, say, your angry part starts to feel more connected and recognizes that the manager that it hated because of how much it tried to stifle the anger is also connected to the larger entity—you. This leads to parts recognizing that when one member of the system is hurt or burdened, it affects the larger system that they all belong to.

If your leg was aching, your hand would automatically move to try to soothe it. As parts come to realize there's a *you* that they're all members of, they're increasingly aware that when one of them is burdened, it affects the whole system. Naturally, they begin to help and care for each other out of that awareness. They become systems thinkers! And they increasingly come to trust Self to lead both inside and outside. Consequently, they support your external altruism with the knowledge that you're not just going to focus out there.

Self recognizes that you and the others are part of a larger body of humanity.

So when people become more and more Self-led, they become increasingly prompted to take action on behalf of healing humanity and healing our planet. At this point in time, there's a critical need for more Self at all levels. Imagine what it would be like if all our leaders knew about Self-leadership and practiced it! This is the kind of larger vision that came to me years ago and has impassioned me ever since. I never thought that I and others could bring it this far in my lifetime, but we've done so much that I've stopped considering it a pipe dream.

Exercise: Fire Drill

So now I want to invite you to try an exercise that will help you experience some of this Self-leadership I've been talking about. I want you to start by thinking of a person in your life (past or present) who really triggers you. Maybe they make you angry or sad, or maybe they're somebody you closed your heart to at some point.

In your mind's eye, put that person in a room by themselves so that they're contained and can't get out right now. Now look at the person through some kind of window, and while you watch the person from outside—from the safety of not being in that room—have them do or say the things that upset you, and notice what happens in your body and your mind as your protector jumps in. That is, notice what your protector does to your muscles, to your heart, and feel what kind of impulses you have. Check out your breathing too. We're just noticing the impact of a protective part on your body and mind.

Now take another look at the person from this place and get a sense of how they look to you through the eyes of this protector. Reassure your protector that you're not going to go into that room, so it can stand down a little. See if it's willing to separate its energy from you, because you're not going to put yourself in jeopardy right now. And if it's willing to pull its energy out of you, you'll notice a palpable shift in your body and your mind as that happens.

What are your muscles like now? What's your heart like? Your breathing? Also pay attention to what's going on in your mind. And then take another look at the person in the room to see if they appear any differently. What does the person look like now?

Then focus again on the protector who jumps up when you focus on this person. See if you can become curious about it now that it's separated from you a little more. And if you can, ask the protector why it feels such a need to become so strong with this person. What's it afraid would happen if it didn't do that for you?

In answering that question, it's likely that it told you about vulnerable parts that it protects, so see if you can show appreciation to it for working so hard to try to keep those parts of you safe. See how it reacts to your appreciation. Ask it if you could heal those parts so they weren't so vulnerable to this person, would it have to be so involved in protecting them? What might it like to do instead inside of you?

We're not going to go into the room holding that triggering person in this exercise. However, I want you to get a sense of what it would be like if you did. If you entered that room feeling more Self-led, what might that look like? How would it play out in terms of how you would relate to this person?

If that's difficult to imagine, it might be because your protector still doesn't trust that it's safe to let you do that. If you *do* have a sense of how different the experience would be, convey that to the protector and ask what it would take for that part to trust you to lead with triggering people like this one. And if it's still afraid to trust you, ask for more information about that.

When the time feels right, thank this part for whatever it did. Show it appreciation for whatever it allowed you to do or let you know. Finally, begin to shift your focus back outside, and take deep breaths if that helps.

In this exercise, if your protector did step to the side, you probably noticed a big shift. In your conversation with the protector, you probably did learn something about the parts it protects and how vulnerable they are. And because those vulnerable parts weren't healed by that exercise, it's likely that it's not going to trust you until they are healed, but it's still interesting to learn about why it doesn't trust *you* to handle people like that.

You may also have noticed when the protector stepped out, that your body felt different and the person in the room looked different. Maybe they didn't look quite as menacing, maybe you could see some of the pain that drove them to do whatever harmful things they have done.

Exercise: Sad Person Meditation

Here's a similar exercise I'd like you to try. Instead of a triggering person, I want you to think of a different person who you've been with when they were very upset—extremely sad and hurt, for example, and maybe crying. Take a second to think of this person and, as before, put them in the contained room. Watch them through the window as they demonstrate how hurt or sad they are.

As you watch them, just notice what comes up in your body and your mind. Notice the thoughts you have about them (even if you're not very proud of those thoughts), and notice all the different parts that react to this person. Feel how these parts affect your body. What are they doing to your heart or your breathing? Your muscles, your impulses? You might notice parts who are making it hard to watch the person in the room. Maybe they feel powerless, want to withdraw, run away, keep your heart closed, or are active in some other way that seems protective.

Pick one of those parts and get to know it better. Let it know that right now you don't have to do anything for this person and that they're going to stay in the room. It can relax a little bit and separate if it can. If it does, notice the palpable shift and look again at the person through these new eyes and get a vision of how you might want to be with this person if your parts would allow it.

As before, shift your focus back to the protector and ask it what it's afraid would happen if it didn't do this to you inside. Why doesn't it trust you to stay with the person? And when this part of the exercise feels complete, you can thank this protector for its work and begin to shift your focus back outside.

These two exercises are examples of how we go about fostering Self-leadership. I use what I call a *constraint releasing approach* to accessing Self. Instead of trying to instill good qualities in a process some call *resourcing*, I have you notice the parts that interfere with your access to Self and then get to know those parts and help them trust you (your Self) to handle difficult people.

If this were a full IFS session, I'd have you get permission to go to the parts those protectors are taking care of and heal them. When you do that, your protectors become much more likely to trust your leadership.

Often your protectors don't trust you with the difficult task of protection, because they think the Self is too tender and is only capable of caring and compassion. My experience is that the Self is adept at all of the C-words that are related to being nice to people, including clarity, confidence, and courage. So when you see through the clear eyes of your Self that someone is doing something hurtful to your parts, you don't have to turn them into a monster. That clarity empowers you to see that their actions arise out of their own hurt, and you also can better see without confusion the damage they do to your parts. This means you have the courage and confidence to set boundaries with them in an effective and, if necessary, very forceful way.

It's important to help your parts trust that they really can rely on you to deal with people and set boundaries that'll protect them and that, actually, if they trust you to do it, the effect will be more powerful and effective. Ideally, this is what the martial arts foster—protection from a nonattached but powerful place. As you enter triggering situations, it's interesting to notice what happens in your body and your mind. You'll start to notice trailheads, which will enable you to learn about the parts that feel a need to protect. If you have access to a therapist or skilled practitioner of IFS, you can then actually go through all the healing steps with support. As you do so, your parts will gradually come to trust you more and won't be so triggered in the future.

Immanence and Transcendence

I want to conclude this part of the book by exploring some of the promises of Self-leadership in a little more depth. To begin with, once you retrieve your exiles and liberate your protectors, you feel more. This is not just because you become more embodied, it's also because you reexperience many of the emotions you felt in childhood but thought you'd left behind when you became an adult. That means you can feel more of your former exiles' awe, joy, and empathy, but also their pain and fear. That's good news, however, because being Self-led means you know how to comfort those parts better, and their feelings don't overwhelm you nearly as much as they once did. You're less detached and more invested—you truly care about what happens on this plane.

At the same time, you've likely had enough experiences with the wave state of Self to know that there is much more to the universe than what happens inside of you, and that in the grand scheme of things, everything is okay. In that sense, you become less attached to what happens on this plane.

Being Self-led means honoring both of these truths equally: *immanence*—fully engaging our humanness—and *transcendence* or liberation—knowing that there's so much more. When we try to deny our vulnerability, we lose touch with our heart. When we fail to realize our divinity, we lose access to our wisdom and perspective. Self-leadership means standing willingly and consciously in both dimensions—feeling the intense emotions of your parts while remaining connected to your transcendent, wave-state awakened mind. If you can hold both in yourself, you can be with both in others.

Some contemplative traditions encourage people to dismiss the concerns of the outside world or withdraw from it as much as possible. For some trauma survivors, this approach has great appeal, because their experience of the world has been harsh and painful, and it's relieving to have some haven from that. While helping you to experience your transcendent Self, some traditions also imply that your personal history (traumas and all) isn't actually all that important—in fact, it's part of your ego's attachment to the mundane world and should be transcended. Through the lens of IFS, this approach only creates more exiles, or pushes the exiles you already have further away. I don't think that any of this is necessary. You can be Self-led and spend time in long retreats or even live as a monastic, and do so without bypassing your exiles.

Activists often rebuke spiritual devotees. Eisenstein articulates the critique like this: "If the house were burning down, would you just sit there and meditate, visualizing cool waterfalls to put out the fire through the power of manifestation? Well, the figurative house is burning down, around us right now. The deserts are spreading, the coral reefs are dying, and the last of the indigenous are being wiped out. And there you are in the middle of it all, contemplating the cosmic sound OM."[7] Of course, the counterargument to this rebuke is fairly straightforward: unless you create a Self-led inner world, whatever you do in the outer world will wind up being protector-led and therefore no different (or, in some cases, worse) than what you're trying to counter.

For this reason, we're after a balance. It's important to fully examine your motives for both inner and outer activities. Are you overwhelmed by the suffering of the world and want to get away from it? If so, you might want to work with your exiles before you find your balance. Are you an activist because you want everyone to know what a good person you are, or because you're driven by burdens from your past?

There's more need than ever for Self-led people to not withdraw, but engage in the world. However, to be Self-led, people have to spend time inside themselves. Many leaders I know, including myself, find an inner/outer rhythm that works well for them. When you can balance immanence and transcendence, you can bring healing to the inner and outer worlds simultaneously.

As David Dellinger writes, "Do you change people first or do you change society? I believe this is a false dichotomy. You have to change both simultaneously. If you're changing only yourself and have no concern for changing society, something goes awry. If you're changing only society but not changing yourself, something goes awry, as tended to happen in the late 1960s. Now, simultaneously may be an overstatement, because I think there are periods when one has to concentrate on one or the other. And there are periods in a society, in a culture, when the emphasis is appropriate only on one or the other. What I'm trying to say is, never lose sight of either the internal world or the external world, the peace within and the peace based on justice on the outside."[8]

Servant Leadership and Contagion

One common objection to doing inner work is that it will make you more egocentric than you already are. My experience is quite the opposite. The more we unburden our parts, the less we need material things or accolades to fill our emptiness. We also feel more connected to others, to our bodies, to our Self, and to SELF.

While I've never needed much materially, during the early years of developing and selling IFS, my exiles craved stroking, and that craving interfered with my ability to convey its power. It's been a big relief in the last decade or so to have healed those parts and offer IFS more from Self. These days people sometimes comment on how humble I am, but genuine humility is hard earned. I did a lot of inner work healing my exiles and, through spending time in the wave state, I've come to realize that IFS isn't about me. I've received it over the years as part of my vision and with the help of so many— in that way, IFS has been a gift and a blessing.

Another name for Self-leadership could be *selfless* leadership, and it sounds a lot like the *servant leadership* model of the business world. Started by AT&T executive Robert Greenleaf, servant leadership "begins with the natural feeling that one wants to serve, to serve *first*. The conscious choice brings one to aspire to lead. That person is sharply different from the one who is *leader* first, perhaps because of the need to assuage an unusual power drive or to acquire material possessions. . . . The difference manifests itself in the care taken to make sure that other people's highest-priority needs are being served. . . . Do those served grow as persons? Do they, *while being served*, become healthier, wiser, freer, more autonomous, more likely themselves to become servants? And, what is the effect on the least privileged in society; will they benefit or, at least, not be further deprived?"[9]

When it comes to *serving*, my primary caution is to be aware of self-sacrificing, caretaking manager parts. Too many leaders have exiled so many other parts of themselves that they become overextended and burn out. Real servant leadership only works when a leader has access to Self and all of their parts. The organization they lead will then reflect the leader's inner harmony and connectedness.

This brings us to the important topic of *contagion* (otherwise known as *resonance*). Protector parts are contagious in the sense that when one member of a system (particularly the leader) is blended with a protector part, it often activates protectors of others, and the culture of the organization becomes permeated with that protective energy. Correspondingly, Self-led people bring out the Selves of those around them. As when one vibrating tuning fork sets off another one at a distance, the presence of Self in a system helps protectors relax and elicits Self throughout the organization.

Earlier I alluded to the phenomenon of resonance in physics and that bears repeating here. Because our particle Self is an aspect of a vibrating field, it will resonate with the Self in other people and with the Self in our parts. Physicists are increasingly recognizing that everything in the universe is constantly vibrating or oscillating at different frequencies, even stationary

The presence of Self in a system helps protectors relax and elicits Self throughout the organization.

objects. They have also noticed that when two things approach each other, they start vibrating at the same frequency—they synchronize.

As a therapist, I try to keep this in mind. I take a minute or so before seeing a client to ask my parts to step back and let me embody, because the success of the session is proportional to how much Self I bring to it. I'm excited to be training senior consultants from international firms like McKinsey, Egon Zehnder, and Mobius to do something similar before they work with their clients. The larger goal becomes to help corporate and political leaders access Self, which will then bring forth the Selves of a company or country such that the field of Self energy permeates the culture.

Flow

Up to now we've mostly been examining how Self-leadership manifests when the Self, in its particle state, becomes the active leader of your inner and outer worlds. When that's the case, you are aware that you are doing something, whether nurturing your parts or protesting injustice. What about when Self is in its wave state? Are there moments when you exist without being aware of yourself or even your Self?

Buddhism refers to such a state as *anatta*, or no-self. These are times when you become so absorbed in an activity that your body moves effortlessly and you lose a sense of separateness. Psychologist Mihaly Csikszentmihalyi coined the word *flow* in the 1970s to describe this state and studied it in a variety of contexts. He found that when people entered flow they found it to be extremely enjoyable and fulfilling, and they performed the associated activity for its own sake rather than for any extrinsic reward.[10] Common examples include the reverie of jazz musicians or other artists who become totally absorbed in their creative process.

I occasionally had experiences like this while playing sports. I would have moments where I'd lose a sense of there being a *me* other than my body moving in a way that was fluid and effective. I played football in college as a defensive back, and there were times when it seemed like time slowed down and I knew exactly what to do without thinking.

I could maneuver around blockers easily, because they seemed to be going in slow motion.

I enter a similar state sometimes when I teach IFS. It's as if words are coming out of me without forethought—almost like I'm channeling something. I feel totally calm, confident, and clear, but without noticing that I'm having those feelings because I'm just being. Those times are also extremely rewarding, which is partly why I teach so much. Afterward I feel glad if people liked the workshop (or me), but that's not my primary motive—I love the flow feeling I get and the sense that I'm fulfilling my purpose in this lifetime.

I believe that flow states are examples of when all your parts are fully aligned with the purpose or pleasure of the activity so their Selves meld with yours. In a sense, they temporarily dissolve, and you are in the nondual wave state—even though you are still operating in this world.

Those flow experiences don't characterize our daily lives, because most of the time we are blended with parts that are working inside to keep us safe, functional, and happy. As you unburden and your parts increasingly trust each other and you, you do feel increasingly integrated and clear about your purpose, so more and more of your life is spent in that unified flow state.

Beyond those flow experiences, many people have had unforgettable moments in their life when they glimpsed pure, wave-state Self. In *The Color Purple*, Alice Walker's character Shug describes her moment: "But one day when I was sitting quiet and feeling like a motherless child, which I was, it came to me: that feeling of being part of everything, not separate at all. I knew that if I cut a tree my arm would bleed. And I laughed and I cried and I run all around the house. I just knew what it was. In fact, when it happen, you can't miss it."[11]

For many people, these glimpses are often life changing. Psychologist Steve Taylor chronicles how people across cultures and time periods describe these experiences in similar ways. Surveys have documented that they are not just confined to the ancients and well-known mystics. It seems that more than a third of us have had at least one such experience, and a smaller percentage have them frequently. Here are some of the similarities people describe:

- A sense that all things are one. "We become aware that, say, a tree and a river—or you and I—are only different in the way two waves of the sea appear to be separate and distinct. In reality they—and we—are part of the same ocean of being."
- An awareness that not only are we connected to everything in the world, but we also tap into a "much more stable, deep-rooted, and expansive self, which can't be damaged by rejection and doesn't constantly hanker for attention and is free of the anxieties that oppress the ego."
- Compassion and love for the people around us, but also for "the whole human race, and for the whole world."
- A new sense of clarity and wisdom that includes the calming sense that everything is okay. "We have the beginning sense that all is well, that in some strange way the world, far from being the coldly indifferent place that science tells us it is . . . is a benign place. No matter what problems fill our life and how full of violence and injustice the world is . . . everything is good, that the world is perfect."
- A vibrating energy that runs through our body and is accompanied by a feeling of intense joy. "This isn't a joy *because* of something . . . it's just there, a natural condition of being."
- A diminished fear of death and the knowledge that death is merely a transition.[12]

I've had versions of these experiences while meditating, but more reliably during ketamine sessions with a Self-led guide. Mary Cosimano, who coordinated Johns Hopkins' psilocybin research for almost two decades and guided almost four hundred sessions, writes that "psilocybin can offer a means to reconnect to our true nature—our authentic self—and thereby help find meaning in our lives. . . . I believe that the nature of our true self is love."[13]

What are we to make of these experiences and their uniformity across people? Many who have them feel that they are communing with God and understand them as mystical or spiritual experiences. On the other hand, some scientifically minded people, like physician Alex Lickerman, interpret these experiences as mere brain activity. "The reason that descriptions of awakening experiences are so uniform ends up being straightforward: the life-condition of Enlightenment is rooted neither in a widespread delusion nor a mystic law or supernatural entity, but rather in the neurobiology of the brain itself. . . . It turns out that all the things that have been found to induce awakening experiences—from meditation to seizures to the use of psychedelic drugs like psilocybin—induce measurably identical changes in the brain."[14]

Self is a spiritual essence within us and around us, like a field, that can quiet that thinking part of the brain.

The less materialistic (and killjoy) interpretation of that neurological observation is that it makes sense that the same brain area shuts down if each of these experiences are openings to pure Self. For me, Self is not a brain state. Instead, it is a spiritual essence within us and around us, like a field, that can quiet that thinking part of the brain. I hope one day to conduct a study in which subjects access Self through IFS and see if the same part of the brain is deactivated.

From my perspective then, these are what Ken Wilber calls "peek experiences," in the sense that we are getting a peek or glimpse of the pure Self that is always there.[15] It's just that it's usually obscured by our parts and their burdens. We are indeed communing with God, if you consider Self to be God within us.

The qualities listed above from Taylor's research are remarkably similar to the eight Cs covered earlier: connectedness and clarity (we're part of the same ocean); calm and confidence (everything is okay); compassion for everyone; and courage (no more fear of death). We can imagine that people also touch the other two Cs: curiosity, in terms of awe at the whole experience, and creativity, in the form of the epiphanies that are often reported.

Do these "peek" experiences of accessing pure Self and feeling connected to everything create a different mindset? Researchers Kate Diebels and Mark Leary developed a brief "Belief in Oneness Scale" and correlated the degree to which a person holds such beliefs with their general values. Their scale used the following six items:

1. Beyond surface appearances, everything is fundamentally one.

2. Although many seemingly separate things exist, they all are part of the same whole.

3. At the most basic level of reality, everything is one.

4. The separation among individual things is an illusion; in reality everything is one.

5. Everything is composed of the same basic substance, whether one thinks of it as spirit, consciousness, quantum processes, or whatever.

6. The same basic essence permeates everything that exists.

They found that those who scored higher on this scale were far more likely to identify with and feel connected to distant people and with aspects of nature than those at lower scores. They were also more likely to have compassion for the welfare of others because of feeling connected to a common humanity, common problems, and imperfections.[16] In other words, experiencing a state of pure Self changes people. As the veils of separateness fall away and they experience the reality of our interconnectedness, they become more Self-led inside and out.

Ralph De La Rosa suggests that at least his version of Buddhism aligns with this position. "It might seem that we have to generate the sense of openness, freshness, joy, revelry, or stillness we touch in such moments. From the Buddhist perspective, however, such a state of being is already there within us and has been so since the beginning. It's tantalizing to think that perhaps expansiveness lies waiting to be uncovered within us while we go searching for it everywhere else. It's not something we go toward so much as it is what we are left with when all our running around ceases. Our deeper nature is simply what's left when we put down the endless task of trying to be somebody."[17]

PART THREE

Self in the Body,
Self in the World

CHAPTER NINE

Life Lessons and Tor-Mentors

We are here to learn a particular set of life lessons, and the lesson plan is already within us. Each of us carries legacy burdens inherited from our families and cultures, and each of us also accrues plenty of personal burdens along the way. So our lesson plan begins with unloading those burdens, and that sets the stage for the most important lesson of all—finding out who we really are.

First, we find out who we aren't. That takes identifying the extreme beliefs and emotions our parts carry that have (often unconsciously) governed our lives, and determining that those don't belong to us. Along the way, we come to know our Self and become Self-led. Needless to say, the journey isn't always unidirectional or smooth.

It took me a while to realize that I'm not worthless and pathetic. Those were just beliefs my exiles carried from being raised by a frustrated father. For years I functioned fairly well in the world, but I had an underlying sense that I was fooling people, and I was driven to achieve in order to counter that suspicion. And when I was with other people, I would avoid dropping my guard out of fear that they would glimpse that real me and blow my whole act to pieces. This went on even after I tasted Self through meditation. In fact, even as I was developing IFS, those exiles would still rush in to remind me of what a pathetic loser I was, especially when I didn't get the positive feedback I was after.

Like many striving achievers, I didn't work with that exile until I was forced to. It took friends in the IFS community to let me know that my protectors were getting in the way of my being a good leader. I finally took their feedback seriously, which was hard. It meant getting to know and unburdening this little boy inside of me who was stuck at a time when my father yelled at him and told him he was "good for nothing."

Most of me already knew I was good for something, but this lonely little guy didn't. After retrieving and unburdening him, he got to learn that lesson, too, and then he was a bundle of inner delight. Correspondingly, when my big achiever part became more relaxed, I could more fully enjoy being alive with the knowledge that, far from being worthless, I was a lovable and loving man. This in-my-bones knowledge gave me more courage to bring IFS into a skeptical world and continues to do so today.

Here's the point of the story: we are sacred beings—as are our parts, as is the Earth. Too many people die without knowing that. Part of what keeps me going is the hope that IFS can change that.

When we know who we are—when we're in Self—we automatically relate to others from those eight C-words and, consequently, we know how to communicate effectively. Good communication involves calm, clarity, creativity, and compassion. Like so many other performance activities, the main challenge is not so much in mastering a particular skill as it is in convincing the managers, who make you self-conscious and afraid of failing, to trust your Self to lead.

We are sacred beings—as are our parts, as is the Earth.

When that happens, it isn't as difficult as it once was to repair broken relationships, because you can better work with the minimizing parts of you or the ones who carry shame. You can reassure those parts in the moment that your mistake doesn't make you bad and you won't be punished the way you were as a child. Additionally, you can be present with the other person's hurt without needing to fix or change it, because you can be present that way with parts of you when they are hurting. The way we relate to our parts translates directly to how we relate to people when they resemble our parts.

In the same vein, if you don't fear your own anger, you'll be able to stay Self-led when someone's angry at you. The person's judgment of you won't trigger your own inner critics, because you know who you are, and because those critical parts of you have retired or taken on new roles. So many of the obstacles in our relationships are because we fear the mayhem that someone else's behavior will create in our inner systems. When Self leads, the mayhem is gone.

> **The way we relate to our parts translates directly to how we relate to people when they resemble our parts.**

Again, I'm not promising you'll be Self-led all the time. But even when you're not, you'll start to notice that you're not. And when a part takes over and you hurt somebody, you know to stop what you're doing, get some space, listen to the part, and come back and speak *for* it rather than *from* it. You speak for your parts from an openhearted place of Self to make a repair with the person you've hurt.

In learning these life lessons and becoming more Self-led, we have the good fortune of having so many excellent teachers out there. I'm not talking about the gurus, priests, professors, or parents, although they can certainly help you learn your lessons if they've learned theirs. I'm talking instead about the difficult events and people that trigger you—your *tor-mentors*. By tormenting you, they mentor you about what you need to heal. That is, the emotions they trigger are usually valuable trailheads. If, instead of blending with those emotions or beliefs, you investigate and separate from them, they will lead you to key exiles like my little worthless guy.

Tor-mentors are so valuable because often you aren't aware of those parts until they or their protectors are activated. Your managers had buried them so far inside that you had no idea. You might have had a nagging sense of them, but your managers found a way to distract you so you wouldn't go there.

I've been lucky to have so many tor-mentors over the course of my life, even if I didn't know it at the time—my parents, for example. A good number of them were actually clients, especially those who were highly sensitive to even the smallest shift in my presence. They had amazing parts detectors. If I was even slightly distracted, impatient, or directive, they would read me the riot act. While these were often overreactions, I learned quickly the futility of trying to point that out, and instead I came to value these episodes. Even if my clients were off the mark about my motives or thoughts about them, usually they were accurately detecting a protector in me that I needed to explore. I would apologize to the client, and I found this to be highly therapeutic, because most of them had intuitions that had never been validated before. And then I'd also work with my own therapist between sessions to help me track and heal the parts I found.

My wife Jeanne deserves a lot of credit for the positive changes people recognize in me over the years we've been together. She has challenged my inconsiderate, narcissistic, and overworking parts in ways that were painful but ultimately healing. We have been outstanding tor-mentors for each other! And I'm proud to say that we still help each other heal that way, especially after big fights.

This is not to suggest that every person or event that gets to you is a valuable tor-mentor. And I certainly don't want to advocate continuing abusive relationships for the purpose of learning some lesson. In that case, the best lesson is probably to take care of yourself and get out of there.

When parts do get triggered, it never hurts to pay attention and take care of them.

Despite kicking off this chapter with the idea that we're all here to learn a particular set of lessons, I've always cringed at the New Age belief that everything that happens is designed to teach you something. I'm also not a big fan of mistaken, Westernized notions of karma. Bad things happen to us that have nothing to do with lessons or with our behavior in this life (or previous ones). That being said, when parts do get triggered, it never hurts to pay attention and take care of them. Maybe one lesson in that is for them to trust you to handle the challenging person or event in front of you, as when I was drowning.

If you take this perspective seriously, then life becomes an interesting series of opportunities to learn that big lesson of who you really are (the acronym AFGO—*Another F'ing Growth Opportunity*—comes to mind). Of course, it's not always that easy to make the U-turn necessary to get the next piece of your curriculum. Your protectors are usually convincing in their message that the tor-mentor in front of you is the real problem, and sometimes, of course, they're correct. But even then, their lesson is to trust your Self to take care of them and navigate the interaction as best you can.

Exercise: Advanced Parts Mapping

You've already done one form of this exercise (Mapping Your Parts) earlier in the book. This is the advanced version, because you'll be using tor-mentors to locate and work with whatever clove of garlic got triggered by the person or event.

Here's a personal example: I was hard at work on a presentation early this morning and suddenly realized that I'd forgotten to join an important call with all of my five brothers to work out some business dealings. There was a lawyer on the call, too, and I was the only brother who didn't make it. I'm the oldest of the six of us, and I wasn't your typical oldest brother in the sense that I was probably the least responsible one. As we were growing up, my father was pretty hard on me about that. I have a critic who can imitate my father pretty well when I screw up, and I immediately noticed that part kicking in today. Although it's changed quite a bit over the years, when I make any type of significant mistake, it still does its thing to some degree. And that always brings up an exile, which means I notice a rush of shame take over my body.

I felt so disappointed after this happened. After all the work I've done on myself, I thought I was beyond that degree of internal reactivity. But since I'm committed to using such episodes to grow, I called the person I trade sessions with right away and used the whole incident as the focus of more healing work.

I tell you this story to inspire you to think of a situation that you'd like to explore more and learn about the parts involved. Before you begin, however, I want to note that you're going to be learning a little bit about the exiles your other parts protect. You won't actually be getting close to the exile, but for some people just learning about their exiles can be triggering. If at any point the exercise feels like it's too much, then pause and step out of the practice and check in with yourself and remind your parts that you're still there. If that helps, then go back in; if it doesn't, then skip this one.

Think of a time when you were quite triggered by something. As you think of that situation, notice the triggered parts and then pick a protector from that clove of the garlic to focus on. Then place your attention on that protector exclusively, finding it in your body or around your body, and notice how you feel toward it. And if you feel anything extreme toward it—you're afraid of it, for example—that's just another part of you, so move your focus to that one for a second.

As we did earlier in the dilemma exercise, notice the two of them—the original protector and the one who has attitude about it—and how they fight inside of you. You can also notice if there are any other protectors that jump in to ally with either side or even take a third position.

So far, we're not interacting with any of these parts; we're just getting a sense of this network that comes up around this trigger in your life. We're getting to know the protectors involved so far. At some point, as you watch this dance of your protectors, see if you can open your mind more toward them so you can learn about them. If you can't get there, that's okay—just spend the exercise noticing. If you do become interested in what all of this activity is about, then go ahead and ask each one about the vulnerability it protects. What does it fear would happen if it didn't take its position?

If your protectors answer that question, you will begin learning about the exiles that drive these extreme responses. And without going directly to those exiles, see how much of a sense of them you can get. Can you guess what they're like? Can you become more aware of their vulnerability?

As you learn more about what your protectors are trying to take care of, it may help you open your heart more to them, because you get more of a sense of what they're dealing with and how high the stakes are. Often, these protectors are like parents who have a highly vulnerable child. They fight and polarize about how best to protect that child, because the stakes are so high if the child were hurt. The difference is that these protectors aren't old enough to be parents—usually they're young themselves, and they're in over their heads just trying to do their best.

What happens in that inner world has tremendous implications for what happens in the outside world.

Let them know you get all that. Tell them you'll keep working with them. And let the exiles know you're aware that they're in there—you can't visit with them today, but at some point, you're going to try to help them too. Remember, what happens in that inner world has tremendous implications for what happens in the outside world.

Now bring your focus back outside and turn your attention back to this external world. You're leaving your internal world, but you're not forgetting it.

For some of you, I suspect that exercise was a little bit difficult, especially as you get to know about exiles. It can be disconcerting to know they're there, and sometimes—even though I said not to go to them—you do get hits of their pain or terror or shame, as well as the kinds of beliefs they carry. That can be troubling for the protectors who've been trying to keep them contained all this time. It's not uncommon to feel a little overwhelmed, and I understand that it can be difficult. Often when we touch an exile even slightly, there's a big backlash from protective parts that are afraid or parts that might now want to criticize you. But if you can keep the perspective that it's just because they're scared, then you can reassure them and help them remember who you are. And maybe that can help you stay grounded.

You are a person who has courage, confidence, clarity, feels connected, and is grounded. If you're feeling anything that tells you you're not, just know that those messages are coming from parts who don't know who you are. Recall that they often believe you're much younger than you are. It's helpful to not totally blend with them and enter their world, but instead reassure them, separate from them, and help them trust that these explorations are hard, but you can do it because you're not a little kid anymore and you're here to help *them*.

Exercise: Working with Triggers

If some of your parts were triggered by the last exercise, here's a practice to help you with that.

Notice what's happening in your body and your mind after having gone into that inner world for a few minutes. If there are any parts triggered by that, rather than blending with them, notice them. As you do so, ask them to separate from you just a little so you can be *with* them without *being* them, and if it's possible to be curious about their triggers from that more separated state, just ask why this was so hard for them. What do they want you to know? And as you're with them and not in them, see if you can reassure them that you're still there. Remind them that you're not young and that you can help them too. You understand that this is hard work and it's scary for some of your parts, but you're there with them.

As you're with these parts in this compassionate way, just remind them that you've been taking care of them and yourself for a long time. You have some wisdom about how to help everybody feel better and you're going to act on that wisdom. When the time feels right, do whatever helps you shift focus back outside.

I hope you were able to do these exercises and learned something about your protectors and what they protect. When I work with couples and they get into conflict, I'll have each of them stop, focus inside, and go through some version of these practices. I do the same when my wife and I get into it. We'll both pause, get a little time to ourselves, focus inside, find the parts that are doing the talking, listen to them, pay attention to what they're protecting, and then come back to each other and speak *for* those parts from a more openhearted place. When we can actually do that, it makes a tremendous difference. We don't always succeed totally, but generally it goes much better than when I let my protectors take over and do the talking.

Too many interactions are protector wars. We see it in corporations, families, and politics. Countries like the US become full of polarizations because the parts of each side take over and do the talking to each other. When one part gets extreme, it makes the protector in the other person become equally extreme, or even more, and the whole dynamic just escalates over time. And that's particularly true when neither side trusts the overall leadership and has a lot of exiles. This is true at all levels of human systems.

Too many interactions are protector wars.

I lead trainings for mediators, conflict resolution experts, and social activists who all find this process helpful. Language like "A part of me got very triggered by what you just said and beneath that part of me was a part that felt hurt" conveys a much different message than "I really don't like what you just said." It also leads to predictably different results. Being Self-led and representing our parts is not just about spending time in our inner world. It's also about how we live in the outer world and relate to other people and their parts.

CHAPTER TEN

The Laws of Inner Physics

A *Beautiful Mind*—a movie about the famous mathematician John Nash—begins with the viewer not understanding that everything they're seeing is through the eyes of a paranoid part of the main character. It's a wonderful example of what people experience when protectors thoroughly blend.

At some point, Nash separates from his paranoid part (Parcher, played by Ed Harris) and along with him, we realize that it's just a part that has taken over his mind. Ignoring Parcher and keeping him at bay helps Nash function, which he does well the rest of his life. For me, this illustrates how helpful mindfulness practices can be.

In IFS, we'd take another step. We'd go to Parcher to learn about what he's protecting. At the end of the film, Nash looks at Parcher, who's staring back at him from across a field where he's standing with a bunch of little kids. They all look at Nash forlornly as he moves on with his life and leaves his protector and exiles in the dust.

All of your parts are in there waiting for you. They deserve your love and attention. But before getting close to the parts we're most afraid will overwhelm us with raw or raging emotions, we've learned to ask those parts to not totally flood us, reassuring them that by not overwhelming us, we're more likely to listen and help them. It turns out that whenever a part agrees to not overwhelm, it won't overwhelm. This is one of the laws of inner physics.

This law enables you to get close to exiles without becoming them. You might feel some of their feelings and blend with them to a certain degree, but they won't take you out in the way they have in the past when that agreement's in place. And that agreement has never been violated in all the years I've been doing IFS.

As it turns out, parts can control how much they overwhelm. This is hard for people to believe, because so often when they open the door to their exiles, they become flooded with all those feelings and they don't feel like they have any control over it. The same is true of protectors at times. As we found in some of the exercises, they can totally blend with you such that you see through their eyes and think the way they think.

This particular law of inner physics has proven extremely valuable in our work with highly delicate, traumatized, or heavily diagnosed clients who are terrified of being overwhelmed by their parts, particularly their exiles. It allows us to enter such inner systems without using the grounding skills that characterize other trauma approaches. Again, it turns out that all we need to do is ask a part to not overwhelm. If it agrees not to, it won't. Parts overwhelm when they believe—often with good reason—that they have to totally take over or we'll lock them away again. It's the same with human exiles.

If a client becomes overwhelmed—has a panic attack in my office, for example—it's because we hadn't made that agreement with the terrified exile in advance. When that occurs, I don't ask the client to take deep breaths, look into my eyes, or feel their feet on the floor. I simply say something like, "I see that a really scared part is here now, and I'd like you to let me talk to it directly." Then, as I talk to that part, I'll let it know that it's very welcome and I'm happy it's been able to break out. I also let it know that it will be a little easier for us to help it if it wouldn't mind separating its energy just a little bit, so that my client can be with it too. Most of the time, the panicked part believes me, and suddenly my client feels grounded, accesses their Self again, and experiences compassion for the panicked part. And they can be *with* the part rather than becoming it.

If Nash had come to see me for a session and started talking about all the people who were out to get him, I'd ask if I could talk directly to the part that was telling him those terrible things. He might initially protest that it wasn't a part, that it was him, but I can be persistent. If he then let me talk directly to Parcher, I'd ask what he was afraid would happen if he didn't take over, and I'd assure him that if he'd let Nash be with him, we could heal whatever he was protecting inside. It might take several sessions before Parcher trusted me enough to separate, but once he did, Nash would see him rather than *be* him, and Nash could honor him for his efforts to protect and we'd be on our way to heal the exile Parcher was trying to deal with.

This particular law of inner physics has been invaluable. I'm covering it here in such depth to assure you that if one of your exiles or protectors takes over during an exercise, it's possible to talk them into separating again.

There's another related law of inner physics I want to mention here, and you'll find it illustrated in some of the transcribed sessions included in this book. There's nothing inside of you that has any power if you are in Self and not afraid of it. This law has also never been proven false in the decades I've been doing this work, and keep in mind that I have worked with clients who have parts that are extremely intimidating and are even determined to hurt or kill them or someone else. And then we do our work together and parts that clients have been afraid of most of their life—parts that feel like actual monsters or demons—suddenly can't do anything to them. The part's usual attempts to control or intimidate now seem feeble, because the client sees what the part is all about, and they see how that part had been stuck in a role.

> There's nothing inside of you that has any power if you are in Self and not afraid of it.

Having said that, it's also important to know that if a person *is* afraid, these parts often carry nasty burdens and can have a lot of power to make people hurt themselves and others. So being in Self and not overrun with fear is crucial. It's also important to remember that the parts aren't what they seem to be, and if you can stay centered with them, they'll reveal their secret histories of how they were forced to be in these extreme roles. They'll also let you know what they're protecting inside, after which you can help those parts transform too.

For me, there's something spiritual about this second inner law. If Self is indeed a drop of the divine within, then it makes sense that unblended Self wouldn't be intimidated by anything—including apparent evil—in the inner world, and instead would work forcefully (but also lovingly and effectively) to heal and transform it.

Check-In

At this point you have encountered nearly all of the exercises in this book. Accordingly, I want to extend some advice or perspective.

First of all, if you've gone on any of these suggested journeys, you may find that your inner system is in a bit of turmoil. You've had the courage to test-drive a different and countercultural way of knowing yourself and relating to your parts that can be quite disconcerting at first. This is particularly true if you are alone with it—if the people around you don't understand and have trouble supporting it.

I want to honor your courage and remind you how important it is to take care of yourself (and your parts) as you continue on this journey. This includes being patient with their skeptical or distressed reactions. Be sure to hold lots of inner meetings and discussions and remind your parts of who you are and who you aren't and how much you care for them and can help them.

This also means listening to what you can do in the outside world that would help them. That might include more distance from some people and more connection to others. It could mean more time out in nature, practicing yoga and soothing meditation practices, taking Epsom salt baths, or watching the kinds of films or TV shows that your parts like (which may not always be your cup of tea). Generally, if you listen, they'll tell you what would help. When neuropsychiatrist and IFS trainer Frank Anderson does medication evaluations, he has patients ask inside if their meds are helping or not. Their parts will let him know how to adjust the dosage or change the medication itself.

I mention these self-care suggestions now because the next exercise can be particularly disconcerting.

Exercise: Advanced Protector Work

We have a motto that all parts are welcome. That being said, there are some parts that we're more afraid or ashamed of.

As you've done in earlier exercises, take a second to get comfortable. If it helps you to take deep breaths or set up as if you're going to meditate, please do that. Start by touching base with the parts you've already been working with. See how they're doing and remind them that you're there with them and that you care about them.

I believe that you can't grow up in the US or other countries with a long history of racism and not carry that legacy burden (although I do find that people from some countries don't carry it). No matter what your race is, no matter how much anti-racism work you've done, it's still likely that there's a part of you that still carries that burden. I love a story that Desmond Tutu tells about getting on a plane and feeling proud to see that there were two black pilots. However, during the flight, there was some technical trouble, and Tutu caught himself worrying that there wasn't a white pilot!

That's just to point out that racism is in all of us. And if we respond to that part by shaming it into exile, we just create more implicit racism, which means even more blind spots and keeping the larger system of racism spinning.

So, that's the part I'm inviting you to look at—the racist. The one who harbors white supremacist beliefs and says nasty things in your head at times. I've done this practice with lots of people, and I find that even those who honestly aren't aware of their own racism at first will find it if they are patient.

I'm not asking you to get close to that racist part. I just want you to notice how you feel toward it. And when another part speaks up—particularly a part that tells you to be ashamed or afraid of your racist part—just let that protector know that letting you get closer to the racist part will actually help it change, and tell them that their exiling approach doesn't really work.

For now, it may be enough to acknowledge the racist part's existence and commit to doing more work with someone who can help you. Here are some reminders from the IFS perspective to help:

- That inner racist is just a part of you. Much of you isn't that way.
- It's not some unworkable bundle of racism. Like all your other protectors, this part can unburden and transform too.
- There's no shame in having this part. Racism is a legacy burden that's pervasive in this culture.
- If you're like me and a number of people I've worked with, this legacy burden permeates many parts, so don't be disappointed if it doesn't totally disappear after you unburden one of them.

Eventually, you may find that this racist part is a protector and you need to heal the exile it protects before it will unburden. Or the part might simply be carrying the cultural legacy burden of racism and it will be more than willing to unload it when you let it know that's possible.

As usual, when you feel you've reached a stopping place, thank your parts for all they've done, and come back to the outside world. Do whatever it takes to ease out of this work and to take care of yourself.

My parents were active in the civil rights movement and I've considered myself active or at least supportive of progressive movements all my life. Yet when I decided to work more directly on issues of racism, I found myself mortified to find a racist part inside of me. I'm not sure why, but it's been one of the toughest parts for me to unburden, and I still get hits of it at times and have to gently counter that part's impulses and beliefs. It's so young and scared. I think it's the same for a lot of people, and one of my goals here is to depolarize the discussion around racism in order to promote more openness and disclosure about what's really going on inside of us.

Until you can unburden your racist parts, it's far better just to be aware of them. If you find one, you can actively remind it, in a compassionate way, that you know it carries those beliefs, but what it says and thinks isn't right. The problem arises when you go to war against your inner racism. As I've said a number of times in this book, going to war against a part usually just strengthens it. When you exile it and pretend it's not there, usually you're just doing it to feel better about yourself, making it much harder to unburden it and counter the potential harm it might do.

I encourage you to use a similar process with other parts you are ashamed of or fear—maybe the one that gives you embarrassing sexual fantasies, or the one that thinks Donald Trump is great, or the part that secretly delights when your friends fail, or the one who believes that men actually *are* superior to women. We all have parts we don't want to admit to, even to ourselves. In general, these parts of us are young and misguided inner children. And just like misguided external children, they deserve to receive our guidance and love, rather than our scorn, shame, and abandonment.

Session Four: Andy

As you might have guessed, I'm excited by the possibility that IFS can help unload inner racism as well as the burdens of denial or apathy—anything that's an obstacle to our appreciating the suffering that systemic racism has caused and acting to counter and repair that damage. I've been experimenting with a number of groups and individuals, and this session is included here to illustrate some of that work.

In a recent podcast, Andy—the interviewer, who is white and very involved in anti-racism activities—allowed me to work with his racist parts.

DICK: Andy, if you were up for it, it'd be great to work with that part of you that's racist.

ANDY: I am open to it. It feels edgy and vulnerable, but I wouldn't be walking the walk if I wasn't open to it.

D: All right, then focus on that part of you that carries racist beliefs and maybe says some racist things in there sometimes and see if you can find it in or around your body.

A: I think it may be two parts—one that's around my mouth and lips, and another one that's harder to find.

D: Okay, let's check in first with the one around your mouth and notice how you feel toward it.

A: He's maybe five or six and in a particular memory. I feel some compassion toward him.

D: Let him know that and see how he reacts and if he wants you to know more about that scene.

A: The scene is in a restaurant with someone I love and trust very much and it's the first time I've seen a black person—I grew up in the suburbs and I lived a sheltered life there—and so I asked this person I was with why that man's skin was dirty. It was just a child's curiosity, but the adult I was with was very embarrassed by that and wrenched away from me and apologized to the black man and told me not to ask questions like that anymore. And what this part is telling me today is that he still fears how his curiosity might hurt that adult and might hurt people with skin that man's color.

D: Ask if he still lives back in that scene.

A: No, but he still worries that those two people are not okay.

D: Okay, then go back there with him and help him see how they're doing and what they need. Now ask him what he wants you to do back there with him or for him.

A: He just wants those two men to connect—the man he loves and trusts and the black man, so I'm helping that happen. He's really happy about it! Now it feels complete.

D: Okay, then let's take him out of that scene to a place he'd enjoy and see if he'd like to give up the beliefs and feeling he got from that time.

A: Yes, very much so.

D: Where's he carry all that?

A: It's in his throat. [*Andy's boy lets it all go out of his throat into the light. The boy feels happy and light and brings courage into his body and the knowledge that adults are hurting, too, and he can help adults connect.*]

D: You mentioned a more elusive one. See if you can find it now.

A: It's kind of hard to describe, but the image that's coming through is of a snake or rope that's coiled around my spine.

D: How do you feel toward it?

A: Kind of scared of it.

D: There's a rule in this work that nothing can hurt you if you're not afraid of it, so see if the scared ones can go to a safe waiting room so we can get to know this snake.

A: Okay, now I feel curious about it. It's letting me know that it's afraid to let me see it.

D: Ask it about that—what's it afraid would happen?

A: It's afraid that a lot of the people I love and care about would be hurt and they would hurt us in return. So it feels better to be invisible. That's why it's been coiling up and hiding. Sometimes it thinks things about people based on how they look—the color of their skin, their facial features—and it knows that that is hurtful.

D: Tell it that we're gonna help it unload whatever makes it think those things—we're not going to have it say anything hurtful to anybody.

A: This part has been around since I was thirteen as a result of having been treated as an exile when I was in middle school because of my weight, my odd interests, who I hung out with, and who wouldn't hang out with me. One defense he developed was to always find a way to feel better than other people. He was really poorly treated for a long time and had to burrow inside.

D: Let him know you're getting this—it makes a lot of sense that he would start judging others just to feel better about himself. [*The part shows Andy a particular scene in the lunchroom where he and his group of friends were disdained by a popular girl and he shrank*]

*and felt humiliated and angry. Andy enters the scene and helps the boy
see that her act had nothing to do with him and goes and talks to the
girl for him. The boy is blown away, because he believed that you can't
stand up to popular people, and once Andy does that for him he's ready
to leave and Andy takes him out to the present.]*

D: See if he's ready now to unload everything he got from those times.

A: Yeah, he's ready—it's hunched in his shoulders and neck. He can't
look straight at people and has to turn his head.

D: What does he want to give all that up to?

A: Fire. *[The boy unloads all that was in his shoulders into the fire and now
is standing a foot taller. He can see how if he were to act toward someone
else the way the girl was to him, he could have that conversation with
them and apologize. "Watching me do that with the girl was eye-
opening for him," he says. The boy then brings self-confidence into his
body and what he describes as "the ability to see that girl's pain and how
she was trying to feel better by shitting on us."]*

D: So, Andy, tell each of these two parts you're going to be checking
on them every day for a while and come on back.

In this short time period, Andy met two parts that are relevant to his
anti-racism work. The first carried a lot of fear of being curious and open about
people of other races—a fear that Andy had to work hard to overcome in his
activism. The second part was using racism to feel better
about himself in an "at least I'm better than those people"
kind of way. In exploring territory like this, I find parts
have many different motives for holding on to racism or
for not getting involved in countering it, but all the parts
I've worked with so far (including my own) are young,
stuck in difficult scenes, and relieved when they unburden.

**I find parts have
many different
motives for
holding on to
racism or for not
getting involved
in countering it.**

Again, here's one central tenet of IFS at work: going
to war against inner beliefs or emotions of any kind will
often backfire. Listening and healing them is the better way to go, all while
relating to them with firm yet loving Self-led discipline until they unburden.

In the process of exploring what seem to be your dark sides, you may also encounter something that doesn't seem like a part. We occasionally encounter voices or images that are quite nasty, but they're also more two-dimensional than parts. We call these things *unattached burdens* because they seem like internalized pieces of hatred or evil that never attached to a part—they're more like free-floating burdens. These are what some psychodynamic systems call *introjects*. But again, one of the laws of inner physics is that if you're in Self and don't fear a part, it has no power over you.

CHAPTER ELEVEN

Embodiment

When your parts start to trust your Self, they open more space for you to be in your body. When that's the case, you feel sensations and emotions more and, consequently, you become increasingly interested in keeping your body grounded and healthy. With this enhanced sensitivity to your body's feedback comes increased knowledge about what foods or activities are beneficial and which can be damaging. This leads to corresponding changes in your behavior. In addition, your exiles no longer have to use your body to try to get your attention or punish you for ignoring them, because they can get through to you directly. I've had many clients resolve chronic medical problems by simply listening to what their bodies were telling them rather than trying to kill the messenger.

Some spiritual traditions diminish the importance of the physical form and even consider the body to be an obstacle to enlightenment. That is, they teach that the needs and drives of the body keep you attached to the material world, whereas the ultimate goal is to transcend it. Others go further and demonize the body and its carnal impulses. But some view the body as a sacred temple that should be carefully attended to because it's the temple of spirit. That's more like how we think of the body in IFS.

A major goal of IFS is for you to increase your ability to be Self-led in both your inner and outer worlds. The more that Self exists in both of those realms, the more the beings in both will become reconnected, harmonious, and balanced. To fully operate in the inner and outer worlds, however, Self needs access to your body. Self needs to be embodied.

If your parts allowed you to do the path exercise in part 2 of the book, it's likely you had a glimpse of this increased embodiment that I'm talking about. And if they weren't as cooperative, usually they have some good reasons from the past for *not* letting you back into your body.

To fully operate in the inner and outer worlds, Self needs access to your body.

People disembody for any number of reasons, but trauma tops the list. When you face a particular trauma, your parts mistakenly believe that they need to protect your Self, so they push your Self out of your body, which is why so many trauma survivors describe watching themselves being hurt from outside (and usually above) their bodies. Thereafter your protectors come to fear re-embodiment because they remain frozen in the trauma scene and believe you're the age you were when the trauma happened, so they often think they're protecting a very young being.

And then, the burdens you accrue from the trauma seem to be dense energy in this inner world and they take up a lot of space inside, so not only is the Self disembodied but these other kinds of energies make it harder for you to re-embody. As a result, most of us live in a less than fully embodied way, which means we aren't bringing optimal levels of Self-leadership to our inner and outer worlds.

As I mentioned before, I played football through college. As a result, I experienced countless head-on collisions, some of which resulted in concussions. I was quite small for football and I played defense, which meant I often had to run full speed into a running back who was much bigger than me and equally fast.

It took years of inner work to get to the point where I could feel my emotions and sensations in my body in the way I could before football—and I wasn't all that sensitive before football. My father had undiagnosed PTSD from World War II—he was a captain of a medical unit in Patton's army and was put in charge of rehydrating all the survivors of Dachau when the camp was liberated. He would tremble with rage when he spanked me.

I parlayed the anger I felt from those experiences to the football field. When that rageful firefighter took over during a game, I could knock players down with no regard for the consequences to my body. Indeed, I would hardly feel my body—only long after the game was over would I feel the bruises. The sense of power, the adrenaline rush, the release of rage, and the accolades from my teammates were all a potent combination. In retrospect, I can understand why our firefighters are so potent and addictive. The accolades took care of my worthlessness; the power, adrenaline, and rage made the weak little boy in me feel strong and alive. Long after my football career was over, I retained an intense desire to run into someone and knock them down.

Parenthetically, a part of me wants to be balanced when it comes to my father. I got a lot of good qualities from him too. He was a true scientist, he was courageous in his field of endocrinology research, and he had an intense commitment to help the world. All of these are also legacies that have influenced my path. And my father could also be very warm, which made things more confusing as a boy when he would fly into his rages.

Another reason that protectors keep you disembodied is that being in your body gives your exiles more access to you. When protectors keep you at least slightly dissociated, numb, or in your head, you never have to feel the exiles' emotions, which means they're less likely to get triggered. That's why it's often a tough sell to get permission from protectors to re-embody.

They correctly fear that you'll feel a lot more, and they worry that it will be too much for you, because they often believe you are still quite young and in jeopardy. Additionally, your protectors have more power to dominate your life when your Self isn't embodied, and they'll resist your embodiment attempts if it means giving up that power to protect.

Indeed, it's the protectors who often convince you to medicate. Medications often have a disembodying effect, which is why they can reduce certain symptoms. When you're medicated, your firefighters calm down, because you aren't as triggered—you don't feel as much. However, since your Self is less embodied, it is harder to do much healing. This is not to say that psychotropic medications aren't helpful, and there are clearly times when your system just needs to chill out for a while. That being said, try not to be disappointed if you can't do much inner work when you're on them.

Of course, some medications—particularly the psychedelics I discussed earlier—can actually relax protectors and allow you to access more Self. Meditation is like this, too—some forms can bring you more into your body, but others are often employed by protectors to keep you more disembodied. For this reason, it's always valuable (and often surprising) to inquire among your parts as to whether a medication or meditation is more or less embodying of your Self. Are you using it to promote healing or to bypass your exiles?

Others reasons for disembodiment include unhealthy diets, lack of exercise, addiction to devices, and the over-busy and over-worked American lifestyle. Relatedly, obsession with your body's size and appearance—our legacy burden of body shame and appearance consciousness—leads to more dieting and constant self-scrutiny, which is also disembodying.

We're sold on any number of solutions that tell us to get more exercise, eat healthier, slow down, and meditate more. These can all be beneficial practices to help us re-embody more, but unless our parts are fully on board, they will ultimately sabotage our healthy solutions. Once we heal our exiles and become more Self-led, we don't have to work so hard to do things that are good for us—we just naturally enjoy them. Our protectors stop driving our bus (they're too young for a driver's license anyway) and let us into the driver's seat. Thereafter, they can help navigate or alert us about dangers in the road or the speed limit, but they'll trust us to drive, while our former exiles play in the back seats.

While you're out of the driver's seat (and sometimes even kicked off the bus), your parts run rampant. They have access to your body for *their* purposes, and the extreme emotions that they carry will affect your body. For example, your managers' fear will make your muscles chronically tense, particularly in your back, shoulders, forehead, and jaw. They're struggling to control how you look, behave, speak, and feel, just as they're struggling to keep your exiles and firefighters contained.

Unless our parts are fully on board, they will ultimately sabotage our healthy solutions.

A number of abuse survivors I've worked with have managers who hate their bodies. They blame their bodies for having needs and keeping them vulnerable, for making them an attractive target. They say, "Those needs got you hurt, so I'm going to numb you out so you don't have those needs anymore." Some try to make them sexually unattractive or unnoticeable so that they become invisible to predators. Or they might encourage them to starve in order to control their appetites and minimize their needs.

It makes sense, in a way, that managers try to control your firefighters, because many of them—like my football-loving part that longed to keep running into people—are adrenaline junkies. They pick activities that release hormones that make you feel high or powerful or even frightened, depending on how they're trying to distract or protect you. But some firefighters take a different approach—they're lazier. They forgo the exertion and get you to consume drugs and foods that have a similar impact.

In the fire drill exercise, you looked through a window at a person who triggers you. I had you feel into your body when a protector took over and notice the effects that had on your body. It's also important to keep in mind that parts still impact your body in their nontriggered states, because they remain frozen in triggering places in your past. Many firefighters retain the ability to take over so thoroughly because you've relied on them in the past, you've established the habit of letting them take over, and they've become associated with the powerful hormones you needed during the originating event. Your sexual firefighter, for example, can always flood your system with testosterone and make you think of nothing but sex. Even when your exiles are so locked away that you have no conscious experience of them, the pain, shame, terror, and desperation they hold is still in your body, as are the stress hormones like cortisol they're aligned with, so there is still the need for the firefighter. You likely think you're just a highly sexual person, not realizing how hard that part is working to protect you.

I've also found that for various reasons, parts will deliberately target different vital organs or systems of your body when they can't get through to you directly. When you won't listen to a part, it has a limited number of options to get your attention or to punish you if it's angry with you. It could give you nightmares, flashbacks, panic attacks, or screw up your body in even worse ways.

We all have genetic flaws or predispositions and our parts often know about those. Just like in the brilliant film *Inside Out*, it's like our parts have a control panel in front of them and they can push our physical buttons at will. I have a predisposition for migraine headaches and asthma. If I'm in a very dusty room, I'll get a bit of an asthma attack, and that has nothing to do with my parts. However, if for some reason a part wants to, it can push the asthma attack button and take me out. It doesn't happen much anymore, thankfully, partly because I've done a lot of work on that. In a similar way, I think many medical symptoms are at least exacerbated or initiated by our parts when they can't get through to us directly—the more we don't listen, the more severe the symptoms.

I had a role in an arthritis study published in the *Journal of Rheumatology*. We had about thirty-six RA (rheumatoid arthritis) patients go through six months of IFS and compared them to a different group of forty that received educational classes on RA. We had the IFS group focus on their pain, get curious about it, and ask it the kinds of questions that we normally ask parts. The participants were mainly Irish Catholic women who'd never been in therapy before and had active caretaking parts that wouldn't let them take care of themselves. As they listened to the pain in their joints, the parts that were using that pain began to answer their questions with answers like, "You never take care of yourself," and "We're going to cripple you so you can't keep doing this," and "We're going to keep doing this until you listen to us." As the IFS group began to listen to those parts and negotiated with the caretaking parts to share time, their symptoms began to improve. We found a highly significant change in the physical manifestation of the arthritis, as measured by third-party physicians. Some people in the group went into complete remission.[1]

> **When you refuse to listen, you can turn your parts into inner terrorists.**

In other words, when you refuse to listen, you can turn your parts into inner terrorists, and they will destroy your body if necessary. Unfortunately, our medical system—in much the same way as a repressive political system—too often is designed to kill the messenger rather than help us get the message.

Session Five: TJ

I want to offer this next transcribed session to illustrate how parts use our body when we don't listen to them. TJ is a medic in her forties who wanted to explore whether there was something psychological about her chronic back pain following a car accident seventeen years earlier.

TJ: I have been struggling for about seventeen years with low back pain and it's been debilitating. I've pushed through it and exercised before, but I got into a wreck when I was pregnant with my second child. As soon as I move it flares up. Doctors say it's arthritis or something. Everything I have enjoyed doing in my life, like triathlons, is unavailable to me. It feels like my body is betraying me. I've also gained thirty pounds and have a lot of shame about that.

DICK: That is a lot. Is there a place in there you'd like to start?

TJ: I don't know how to deal with the pain. I don't know if the pain is trying to tell me something.

D: We can check that out if you'd like. We're going to be totally open-minded—it may not be anything but a spinal problem. We'll just check. Focus on the pain itself—I assume it's in your back. As you notice it there, how do you feel toward it?

TJ: I don't like it. I'm so mad about it.

D: I understand why parts are angry at it, but I'm going to ask them if we can get a chance to know the pain in a different way and if there's something it wants us to know. So, see if the ones that are angry will give us some space for a few minutes. [*TJ does*] How are you feeling toward the pain now?

TJ: I'm still mad at it.

D: What does the one who is mad need to give us some space? Maybe a voice for a while?

TJ: There's a fear that comes in that doesn't want to look at the anger.

D: Ask the fear what it's afraid will happen if you work with the anger.

TJ: It might unearth some other horrible trauma.

D: What would happen if you unearth something horrible?

TJ: It thinks I won't be able to deal with it or it'll take over.

D: Ask this fear how old it thinks you are.

TJ: I got really young.

D: Let it know you're not really young and see how it reacts.

TJ: It's shocked.

D: Find a way to convince it that you're not really young.

TJ: It's settled now. It'll let us go to the angry one.

D: How do you feel toward that one now?

TJ: Okay.

D: See what it wants us to know.

TJ: There's a critic now. "You're lazy, you don't do anything."

D: So, we need to deal with the critic. How do you feel toward it?

TJ: He is very large. He's so mean.

D: Can all the parts that get hurt by him give us some space? Do you want me to talk to him directly? [*She nods*] Okay, are you there? [*Nods*] So, you're pretty hard on TJ, is that right? Why do you do that to her?

TJ: She's lazy and doesn't do anything and needs to get off her ass. She's fat and ugly and disgusting.

D: What do you fear would happen to her if you didn't say this all the time?

TJ: She would be three hundred pounds, unemployed, and worthless.

D: You're trying to keep her in shape and working.

TJ: I know she has potential to get back to a weight that feels better and healthy.

D: So, is weight your main focus?

TJ: No. Healthy. I want her to do any activity within reason.

D: I get it. Of course, you're frustrated with her back issue.

TJ: It's so bad. I'll get her motivated and then she'll blow everything off because she's in pain.

D: Okay. I get your dilemma. How's the shaming working for you?

TJ: It's not. The shaming makes her eat worse, et cetera.

D: Are you ready to try something different?

TJ: Yes.

D: Would you give us permission to go back to the angry one?

TJ: Yes. [*Pause*] I can't find anger now because it's not allowed. The critic says anger is a worthless emotion and doesn't help.

D: Will she give us a chance to help it? It's not just a bundle of anger, it's a part in a role. Tell your anger it's safe to come back. Let him know you are curious about him and see what he wants you to know.

TJ: A blocker comes in and wipes everything out.

D: Ask it what it's afraid would happen if we stay with the anger.

TJ: It will be ugly. It'll take over.

D: Tell it that's not going to happen.

TJ: Anger is behind bars, should I let him out?

D: Yeah, let him out and see what he wants you to know.

TJ: The blanking comes back.

D: Ask it why it came back.

TJ: It wants to describe what anger looks like. He's a big scary monster.

D: How close are you to anger in terms of feet away?

TJ: A couple feet.

D: Tell your parts that no part has any power if you aren't afraid of it. Tell your scared parts to go to a safe waiting room. [*She does*] How do you feel toward him now?

TJ: Interested.

D: Good. Let him know. [*Long pause*] How does he react? What does he say?

TJ: I'm getting the car accident and the fear of it.

D: Is it okay to be with this?

TJ: Yes.

D: Let him know you really want to get what it was like for him.

TJ: I was pregnant, and my two-year-old was behind me. And I stopped at a red light. There's a judgmental part that says you shouldn't share that, just move on.

D: Put it in the waiting room. Be a little firm with these parts.

TJ: I was talking on the phone because you could still do that and stopped at a light. Out of nowhere, this car slams into the back of us going fifty-five miles per hour. Because it hit so hard, we went up and over and I ended up head to head with the gal that hit us. I just went straight into being a medic. I got my child out of the back and carried her, yelling directives, not realizing my head was bleeding. I was scared that I would have my baby too soon. They gave me drugs that made me crazy in order to stop the labor. It was scary and I felt alone, and I don't think I really ever processed that.

D: See if this angry part needs you to get anything more about it.

TJ: I never got mad at the driver who hit me. I never got to be mad. It was just all about the pain and the worry about my child. I was hurt in several ways. There's something about the mad part and I feel like I need to get there.

D: Let the anger know you are ready now.

TJ: It's in my stomach now. It's so mad [*she starts to shake*].

D: That's okay. Just stay with it.

TJ: There's a part that says it's not okay to be mad, but I'm so fucking mad at her. It wrecked me for so long and still . . .

D: Yeah. It has every right to be angry about that. Let it know that. It's really welcome, it can be as big as it wants.

TJ: Can I stand up?

D: Yeah. Stand up.

TJ: I'm so embarrassed. Okay . . . [*screams at the top of her lungs*].

D: Really great. It's really great that this part can be here now. How do you feel toward it now?

TJ: It's been stuck. Really, really stuck.

D: How is it doing now?

TJ: It's so much lighter.

D: Good. Just ask it if we need to get it out of there, if it's still stuck back there. [*She nods*] Okay, so, I want you to go back into that scene and be with that angry part and any parts that are still there, in the way that they needed.

TJ: They just needed to be heard. It wants me to use my voice.

D: So, what do you say to that?

TJ: It's right.

D: You may need to work with the other parts that don't want you to use your voice. Is it ready to leave that time and place?

TJ: Yes.

D: You can see if there are any other parts stuck back there that want to come along.

TJ: Fear, pain, and anger and the pleasing part all want to go.

D: Take all four of them to a safe and comfortable place. [*After a pause*] Where do you have them?

TJ: In a lodge in the mountains.

D: Are they happy?

TJ: They are.

D: Good. Let them know they never have to go back there, and you'll be taking care of them. See if they are ready to release the feelings from that time.

TJ: They don't believe me that I'll take care of them.

D: Do they have reason not to believe that?

TJ: Yes.

D: Tell them that's another project—that you'll keep working with the parts that are afraid for you to have a voice. See if they are ready to unload the feelings and beliefs they got back there.

TJ: Okay.

D: What do they all want to give it up to? Light, water, fire, wind, or anything else?

TJ: Snow.

D: Tell them to take that out of their bodies and let it go into the snow. Just get it out.

TJ: Okay.

D: How are they all doing?

TJ: They want to party.

D: Tell them to invite into their bodies the qualities they'll need in the future.

TJ: Courage, connection, freedom, voice.

D: How are they doing now? Let's invite in that critic and all the other protectors from along the way and see how they react.

TJ: There's kind of delight. Creativity wants to come back too.

D: Good. Bring creativity back too. Before we stop, can we go back to the back pain to just see how it feels now.

TJ: There is no back pain right now.

D: Ask these guys if they had a role in the back pain.

TJ: Yes, they needed me to listen. It's been a long time.

D: Let them know that if they ever need to get your attention again, that you'll listen. Does that feel complete for now?

TJ: Yes, but anger's saying don't fucking minimize it anymore.

D: How does that feel to hear?

TJ: Not very nice but it feels right.

D: Maybe you can apologize for minimizing things and commit to keep working with the parts that do that. How does that feel now?

TJ: Lighter. Amazed. Thank you.

The next time I saw TJ was a year later when she came to another retreat I was leading. She said she hadn't experienced any back pain since our session. It's important to note that TJ fulfilled her commitment to her parts by continuing to work with them on her own. Had she not done that, the pain would probably have returned.

Exercise: Body Meditation

Here's the last exercise I want to offer, and it's related to these ideas about your body. As you've been reading, you've likely been thinking about your relationship with your body, perhaps about symptoms you've had. So, again, I don't want to presume that any of your symptoms or tensions are necessarily the result of parts. Additionally, I don't want to kick up any shame by suggesting that you're doing all this to yourself. That's not the message at all. It's not *you* who wants to have a symptom, it's just a little part. Often that part has no clue about the overall damage they're doing to your body or to your family, and once you finally listen to that part it will stop doing it to you.

I'm going to invite you now to focus on your body, and if you do have a medical condition, feel free to focus on the manifestation of that. If you don't, then just find a place in your body that doesn't quite feel like you—any spot of tension, pressure, congestion, achiness, or fatigue. We're looking for a sensate trailhead—a point to focus on and begin this exploration. I'll give you a second to find one.

When you have found one, place your attention on it and notice how you're feeling toward it. You may feel frustrated or defeated by it or wish you could get rid of it, all of which are understandable. But for our purposes, we're going to ask those parts to give us a little space so you can just get to know it. And if it is possible to shift into that curious place, ask what it wants you to know.

And again, wait for an answer. All of your thinking parts who want to speculate can relax, and if no answer comes, that's fine. It could be just a physical issue that's not related at all to your parts. If you do get an answer, however, then just stay with the sensation as if it were a part of you and ask it the kinds of questions we ask parts. For example, "What are you afraid would happen if you didn't do this to my body?"

If it answers that question, then you learned about how it's trying to protect you somehow, and you can show it appreciation. But it may be that it's not a protector and that it's just trying to get a message to you. So another useful question here is, "Why do you feel like you have to use my body?" That is, why doesn't it feel like it can talk to you directly? And a final question could be something like, "What do you need from me to not have to do this to my body?"

And again, when the time feels right, you can thank the part for whatever it shared (if it shared anything) and begin to shift your focus back outside, taking deep breaths if that helps.

This is one way to practice a new relationship with your body. Whenever a sensation or symptom comes up, pay attention to it. What message is it trying to send you?

Closing Thoughts

Your inner world is real. Parts are not imaginary products or symbols of your psyche; nor are they simply metaphors of deeper meaning. They are inner beings who exist in inner families or societies, and what happens in those inner realms makes a big difference in how you feel and live your life.

If you don't take them seriously, you'll have a hard time doing what you're here to do. You might be able to unburden your parts to some degree, but it will help you tremendously to enter your inner world with full conviction and treat your parts like the real and sacred beings they are.

If you don't take your parts seriously, you won't become an effective inner leader or parent. Various forms of psychotherapy can help you connect with the deep-seated emotions of your exiles, and that can be healing to some degree. But if you think of that process through the lens of expressing a repressed emotion, you won't follow up—and following up is crucial.

If, on the other hand, you understand that you have exiles who really need to trust you, you'll be more likely to visit them for as long as it takes. Working with them like that is often what's needed to reach permanent unburdening, and that's what it takes to learn your lessons—lessons like *everything deserves love*.

When you can love all your parts, you can love all people. When your parts feel loved, they allow you to lead your life from Self, and you feel connected to the Earth and you want to save it from the exploitive parts of others. You will expand the field of Self on the planet, and that will contribute to healing it. You'll also feel connected to the bigger field of SELF.

When you can love all your parts, you can love all people.

It's challenging to think of parts as real when the mono-mind view of people permeates most of the world's thinking and communication. We constantly ask each other, "What do *you* want?" as if there were only one you. We ask the same of ourselves. Then we say, "*I* want to go out tonight." Although sometimes we might say something like, "A part of me wants to go out and another part wants to stay home," that's not the norm, and even when people talk that way, most don't mean a literal subpersonality. Unfortunately, having many personalities is still highly stigmatized and pathologized.

Earlier in the book, I wrote about the Self being contagious. When you're embodied and you're with another person, not only do they begin to sense the presence of your Self, but their Self also comes to the fore and starts to resonate. Your protectors and theirs will sense the comforting level of Self in the room and will relax, releasing even more embodied Self energy.

I see this all the time when I work with couples, families, corporations, or other organizations. Simply holding people in an embodied state while they negotiate the conflict makes a huge difference. I'll often ask for each person to allow me to be the parts detector, and I'll pause the action when their parts get into it, and then I have everyone—myself included—go inside, listen to their parts, and then come back and speak from an openhearted place of Self on their behalf.

I also believe that countries have parts and a Self and that we can use a similar process with leaders of those countries, and IFS is currently being used by consultants to do just that. Of course, protector parts are contagious too. Most significant polarizations are driven by protectors and their burdens—their extreme beliefs and emotions—and they escalate with protectors in other people. We see this playing out far too often at the international level.

One of my favorite sayings applies here: When the water buffalo battle in the marsh, it's the frogs who suffer. When my protector comes at you, it'll hurt your exile (the frog). And when your protector comes back at me, it hurts my exile, and on and on. Neither of our protectors allows us to let on that we're being hurt—neither of us speaks for those frogs. Instead, we just let our water buffalo keep trampling each other.

When the water buffalo battle in the marsh, it's the frogs who suffer.

The solution to such escalations is for the Self in both parties to call off the water buffalo, to comfort and love our own frogs, and then to have the courage to let each other know about that damage. Once each partner shares their exiles' experience, the atmosphere shifts palpably, and that makes compassionate repairs and win/win solutions possible.

There are parts of us that will try to convince us not to do that. They'll tell us that it's weak and that it's too exposing to show others our true needs. The truth is that genuine strength can only come when we communicate from Self. When we do so, others will sense the power in our vulnerability.

I believe that by caring for our parts in this nurturing way, embodying Self, and communicating in a Self-led way, not only are we creating more harmony inside and between us and others, but we're also bringing more Self energy to the planet. And once there is a critical mass of Self energy in any system, healing happens spontaneously and quickly.

Once there is a critical mass of Self energy in any system, healing happens spontaneously and quickly.

That's what we need. We seem to be living in a crucial time in the history of our species, and the need for a critical mass of Self has never been greater. I used to believe that Self doesn't have any agendas, but I don't anymore. Maybe *agenda* isn't the best word for it, but in my experience, Self does have a purpose or a desire to foster connectedness, harmony, balance, and to correct injustice. But unlike our parts, Self isn't attached to that happening in any particular way, or at least not immediately. Self has more of a wide-angle, long-term perspective.

I believe that your individual Self is part of a larger field of SELF that can harmonize human interactions. Whenever you act from Self or help release it in others, you are contributing to that field's growth and ability to affect the world. This gives more meaning not only to what IFS therapists do in their offices, but also to our small, unwitnessed acts of integrity or compassion—including loving our own inner and outer children.

This field perspective helps us understand how the Self and burdened parts are contagious, because they're all aspects of fields too. And if we view the Earth as a living, sentient organism, it's as if Self has been increasingly obscured by the fields created by the inhumane ways we have treated the planet and each other. When we see right-wing, nationalistic leaders emerge in different countries around the planet who are using the same manipulative and despicable tactics, it's as if those countries are becoming enveloped by the same dark field.

That makes unburdening ourselves and one another all the more important. In doing so, we lessen the power of that obscuring field and strengthen the Earth's field of Self. That takes us working together. We need to build communities of support for these shifts to happen, especially when they're seen as countercultural, because they're hard to maintain on our own. We need to be with people who can let us know we're not crazy even though the rest of the world might disagree. I would not have persisted to create IFS had it not been for the small group of peers who were experimenting along with me and validating each other. If you're curious about learning more, the IFS Institute sponsors many Facebook groups or listservs, as well as an online Circle program.

To summarize, here's what I'm suggesting:

1. We lead our lives from Self as much as possible and find ways to help increasing numbers of people do the same.

2. We heal (unburden) ourselves and one another.

In the same way, I'm convinced that there are ways to help large groups uncover and unburden cultural legacy burdens like racism, individualism, consumerism, materialism, and sexism. That being said, in this larger work, I think it's a mistake to diminish the importance of unloading our individual burdens. Until our parts feel securely attached to us, to the Earth, and to SELF, we will have protectors that crave power, adoration, material things, and status—all the things that keep us separate from one another and keep us unaware of the consequences of abusing the Earth.

There are ways to help large groups uncover and unburden cultural legacy burdens.

None of these changes are possible if we subscribe to the current paradigm of the mind and human nature. It's not enough to simply address specific problems—green energy initiatives, for example—because as long as we continue to view human beings as selfish, separate, and disconnected, we will continue relating to our parts in ways that make them increasingly extreme, and the host of problems we now face will find other ways to manifest. On the other hand, challenges like the coronavirus pandemic and developing ecological crises may break through our denial and sense of cultural superiority enough to make room for a new paradigm.

When we're in Self, we remember our connectedness to our parts, to other people, and to the Earth. We view each other as sacred beings and relate with love and respect. We also remember our connectedness to the SELF and can receive wise guidance from that level of consciousness. In being Self-led, we find our vision naturally and act on it, and in doing so, material things don't seem as important as they once did. We relax and slow down. And we increase the field of Self on the planet and work to reduce the fields of burdens that engulf it.

It's been wonderful to share this fantastic journey with you. Writing this book has encouraged me to further explore, clarify, and consolidate my beliefs about the spiritual side of IFS, and for that I'm thankful. In the process, I've found and worked with several parts of myself—the one who uses my father's voice to hector me about how unscientific all this is, the one who worries that I'm being too grandiose with all of these major pronouncements about the world and how it could be, and the one who still doubts the reality of the inner world, despite decades of evidence.

As I unburden each of these parts, I can feel pure gratitude for this opportunity and for you having enough interest in these ideas to pick up this book and read this far. May you find it helpful in some way, and may the Self be with you!

ACKNOWLEDGMENTS

There are an immense number of people to thank for contributing to the development of the IFS model—far too many for this space. However, for this book in particular, I can identify several key figures. In the early days, I was led—sometimes kicking and screaming—toward spiritual explanations of the phenomena we were encountering in clients by several fellow explorers: Michi Rose, Tom Holmes, Susan McConnell, Kay Gardner, Paul Ginter, Toni Herbine Blank, and the late Ron Kurtz, the developer of Hakomi. Later I enjoyed comparing notes and receiving guidance from a Sufi mystic, Cindy Libman, and for the past decade of trading powerful sessions with Carey Giles. I also want to acknowledge that many of our current trainers are spiritually oriented and have shared in the development of many of these ideas with me.

I've also enjoyed collaborations with Loch Kelly, Lama John Makransky, Lama Willa Miller, and Ed Yeats of the Tibetan Buddhist tradition; and with Christians Mary Steege, Jenna Riemersma, and Molly LaCroix. Bob Falconer did much of the research for our book *Many Minds, One Self*, which also deepened my appreciation of the ubiquity of Self in various spiritual traditions. I also want to thank Bob Grant for guiding the ketamine trips that gave me more conviction about the spiritual aspects of this work.

My early appreciation of systems thinking was strengthened during my time as a student of the late Doug Sprenkle, as well as through collaborations with Doug Breunlin and Howard Liddle. While I never studied with him directly, the late Salvador Minuchin was a major influence on IFS. I learned from the late Reggie Goulding about the impact of trauma on inner systems, and I want to thank Bessel van der Kolk for the pioneering work that validated and fortified those discoveries. I found similar validation in Gabor Maté's work and conversing with him about addiction and medical symptoms.

I feel very well taken care of by Sounds True. They blessed me with a great editor, Robert Lee. Early in the process he caught the vision and put his heart into a major reorganization that improved the book enormously. I'm also grateful for Jennifer Yvette Brown's creativity and Tami Simon's interest and support.

Finally, I want to thank my brother Jon for freeing me up to explore all of this by doing such a good job of running the IFS Institute the past decade, as well as my wife and co-explorer, Jeanne Catanzaro, who has an amazing intuition and made significant contributions to my thinking about these issues.

NOTES

Epigraphs

1. Robert Pirsig, *Zen and the Art of Motorcycle Maintenance* (New York: Morrow, 1974).
2. Gus Speth, as quoted in "We scientists don't know how to do that . . . what a commentary!" WineWaterWatch.org, May 5, 2016, winewaterwatch.org/2016/05/we-scientists-dont-know-how-to-do-that-what-a-commentary/.
3. Thomas Merton, *Conjectures of a Guilty Bystander* (New York: Image Books, 2009).

Introduction

1. Daniel Christian Wahl, "[We Are] a Young Species Growing Up," Medium, January 13, 2018, medium.com/age-of-awareness/we-are-a-young-species-growing-up-3072588c5a82.
2. Jimmy Carter, "A Time for Peace: Rejecting Violence to Secure Human Rights," June 18–21, 2016, transcript posted June 21, 2016, speech at the Carter Center's annual Human Rights Defenders Forum, cartercenter.org/news/editorials_speeches/a-time-for-peace-06212016.html.

Chapter One: We're All Multiple

1. Jonathan Van Ness, *Over the Top: A Raw Journey to Self-Love* (New York: HarperOne, 2019), 5–6.
2. John Calvin, *The Institutes of the Christian Religion: Books First and Second* (Altenmünster, Germany: Jazzybee Verlag, 2015).
3. Rutger Bregman, *Humankind: A Hopeful History* (New York: Little, Brown, 2020), 17.
4. For a thorough review of this and related studies, see Rutger Bregman, *Utopia for Realists* (New York: Little, Brown, 2017).
5. Van Ness, *Over the Top*, 173.
6. Van Ness, *Over the Top*, 261.

7. Ralph De La Rosa, *The Monkey Is the Messenger: Meditation and What Your Busy Mind Is Trying to Tell You* (Boulder, CO: Shambhala, 2018), 5.

8. Matt Licata, *The Path Is Everywhere: Uncovering the Jewels Hidden Within You.* (Boulder, CO: Wandering Yogi Press, 2017), 72.

9. Jeff Brown, *Karmageddon*, directed by Jeff Brown and Paul Hemrend (Ontario, Canada: Open Heart Gang Productions, 2011), documentary, 2 hours.

10. Brian Gallagher, "The Problem with Mindfulness," *Facts So Romantic* (blog), Nautilus, March 30, 2018, nautil.us/blog/the-problem-with -mindfulness; and Lila MacLellan, "There's a dark side to meditation that no one talks about," *Recesses of Your Mind* (blog), Quartz, May 29, 2017, qz.com/993465/theres-a-dark-side-to-meditation-that-no-one-talks- about.

11. Saul McLeod, "Bowlby's Attachment Theory," Simply Psychology, updat- ed 2017, simplypsychology.org/bowlby.html.

Chapter Two: Why Parts Blend

1. T. Berry Brazelton, *Infants and Mothers: Differences in Development* (New York: Dell, 1983).

2. Follow-up correspondence with Sam by the author.

Chapter Three: This Changes Everything

1. Henry Wadsworth Longfellow, *Poems and Other Writings*, ed. J. D. Mc- Clatchy (New York: Library of America, 2000).

Chapter Four: More on Systems

1. Fritjof Capra and Pier Luigi Luisi, *The Systems View of Life* (Cambridge, UK: Cambridge University Press, 2014).

2. University of Liverpool, "Study Finds Psychiatric Diagnosis to be 'Scientifically Meaningless,'" Medical Xpress, July 8, 2019, medicalxpress.com/news/2019-07-psychiatric-diagnosis -scientifically-meaningless.html?fbclid=IwAR07fYCVRQr01 rjrQGn6_dfRCHtELXf2bBeWB-J02t2mXYQRBY5fSsK_8ss.

3. Donella Meadows, *Thinking in Systems: A Primer* (White River Junction, VT: Chelsea Green, 2008), 163.

4. Rutger Bregman, *Humankind: A Hopeful History* (New York: Little, Brown, 2020).

5. Bregman, *Humankind*, 344.

6. Charles Eisenstein, *The More Beautiful World Our Hearts Know Is Possible* (Berkeley, CA: North Atlantic Books, 2013), 107.

7. Meadows, *Thinking in Systems*, 155.

8. Jordan Davidson, "Scientists Warn Worse Pandemics Are on the Way if We Don't Protect Nature," EcoWatch, April 27, 2020, ecowatch.com /pandemics-environmental-destruction-2645854694.html?rebelltitem =1#rebelltitem1.

9. Eisenstein, *The More Beautiful World*.

10. Meadows, *Thinking in Systems*, 184.

Chapter Five: Mapping Our Inner Systems

1. Robert Bly, *A Little Book on the Human Shadow*, ed. William Booth (New York: Harper Collins, 1988).

Chapter Six: Healing and Transformation

1. Michael and Annie Mithoefer, unpublished report.

2. Kathryn Jepsen, "Real Talk: Everything Is Made of Fields," Symmetry, July 18, 2013, symmetrymagazine.org/article/july-2013/real-talk -everything-is-made-of-fields.

3. Tam Hunt, "The Hippies Were Right: It's All about Vibrations, Man!" *Scientific American*, December 5, 2018, blogs.scientificamerican.com /observations/the-hippies-were-right-its-all-about-vibrations -man/?fbclid=IwAR3Qgi8LisXgl-S2RO5mBtjglDN _9lJsVCHgjr0m9HR4gBhO83Vze8UeccA.

4. See Jenna Riemersma, *Altogether You: Experiencing Personal and Spiritual Transformation with Internal Family Systems Therapy* (Marietta, GA: Pivotal Press, 2020); and Mary Steege and Richard Schwartz,

The Spirit-Led Life: A Christian Encounter with Internal Family Systems (Scotts Valley, CA: Createspace, 2010).

Chapter Seven: The Self in Action

1. Charles Eisenstein, *The More Beautiful World Our Hearts Know Is Possible* (Berkeley, CA: North Atlantic Books, 2013).
2. Follow-up correspondence with Ethan by the author on June 26, 2020.

Chapter Eight: Vision and Purpose

1. Wendell Berry, *The Unsettling of America: Culture and Agriculture* (San Francisco: Avon Books, 1978).
2. Jean Houston, *A Mythic Life: Learning to Live Our Greater Story* (San Francisco: Harper, 1996).
3. Abraham Maslow, *Motivation and Personality*, 3rd ed., ed. Robert Frager, James Fadiman, Cynthia McReynolds, and Ruth Cox (New York: Longman, 1987).
4. Scott Barry Kaufman, *Transcend: The New Science of Self-Actualization* (New York: Penguin Random House, 2020), 117.
5. Dan Siegel, *Aware: The Science and Practice of Presence* (New York: TarcherPerigree, 2018), 10.
6. Charles Eisenstein, *The More Beautiful World* (Berkeley, CA: North Atlantic Books, 2013), 59.
7. Eisenstein, *The More Beautiful World*, 85.
8. David T. Dellinger, *Revolutionary Nonviolence: Essays by Dave Dellinger* (Indianapolis: Bobbs-Merrill, 1970).
9. Robert Greenleaf, *Servant Leadership* (Mahwah, NJ: Paulist Press, 1991), 13–14.
10. Mihaly Csikszentmihalyi, *Flow: The Psychology of Optimal Experience* (New York, Harper & Row, 1990).
11. Alice Walker, *The Color Purple* (New York: Mariner Books, 2003).
12. Steve Taylor, *Waking From Sleep: Why Awakening Experiences Occur and How to Make Them Permanent* (Carlsbad, CA: Hay House, 2010).

13. Mary Cosimano, "Love: The Nature of Our True Self: My Experience as a Guide in the Johns Hopkins Psilocybin Research Project," MAPS *Bulletin* Annual Report 24, no. 3 (Winter 2014): 39–41, maps.org/news-letters/ v24n3/v24n3_p39-41.pdf.

14. Alex Lickerman and Ash ElDifrawi, *The Ten Worlds: The New Psychology of Happiness* (Deerfield Beach, FL: Health Communications, 2018), 296.

15. Ken Wilber, *The Essential Ken Wilber: An Introductory Reader* (Boston, MA: Shambhala, 1998).

16. Scott Barry Kaufman, "What Would Happen If Everyone Truly Believed Everything Is One?" *Beautiful Minds* (blog), *Scientific American*, October 8, 2018, blogs.scientificamerican.com /beautiful-minds/what-would-happen-if-everyone-truly-believed -everything-is-one.

17. Ralph De La Rosa, *The Monkey Is the Messenger: Meditation and What Your Busy Mind Is Trying to Tell You* (Boulder, CO: Shambhala, 2018), 6–7.

Chapter Eleven: Embodiment

1. Nancy Shadick et al., "A Randomized Controlled Trial of an Internal Family Systems-Based Psychotherapeutic Intervention on Outcomes in Rheumatoid Arthritis: A Proof-of-Concept Study," *Journal of Rheumatology* 40, no. 11 (November 2013): 1831–41, doi.org /10.3899/jrheum.121465.

ABOUT THE AUTHOR

Richard C. Schwartz, PhD, began his career as a systemic family therapist and an academic. Grounded in systems thinking, Dr. Schwartz developed Internal Family Systems (IFS) in response to clients' descriptions of various parts within themselves. While exploring that inner terrain with traumatized clients, he stumbled onto the discovery of an undamaged, healing essence that he calls the Self, and that led him on the spiritual journey described in this book. A featured speaker for national professional organizations, Dr. Schwartz has published a number of books and over fifty articles about IFS, which has become a global movement. Learn more at ifs-institute.com.

ABOUT SOUNDS TRUE

Sounds True is a multimedia publisher whose mission is to inspire and support personal transformation and spiritual awakening. Founded in 1985 and located in Boulder, Colorado, we work with many of the leading spiritual teachers, thinkers, healers, and visionary artists of our time. We strive with every title to preserve the essential "living wisdom" of the author or artist. It is our goal to create products that not only provide information to a reader or listener but also embody the quality of a wisdom transmission.

For those seeking genuine transformation, Sounds True is your trusted partner. At SoundsTrue.com you will find a wealth of free resources to support your journey, including exclusive weekly audio interviews, free downloads, interactive learning tools, and other special savings on all our titles.

To learn more, please visit SoundsTrue.com/freegifts or call us toll-free at 800.333.9185.